DATE DUE		

Women Who Made a Scene

Remarkable Women: Past and Present

Women Who Made a Scene

Heroines, Villainesses, Eccentrics

Lesley James

RAINTREE STECK-VAUGHN PUBLISHERS
RSVP®

A Harcourt Company

Austin   New York
www.steck-vaughn.com

Published by Raintree Steck-Vaughn Publishers, an imprint of Steck-Vaughn Company

CREATED IN ASSOCIATION WITH MEDIA PROJECTS INCORPORATED
C. Carter Smith, *Executive Editor*
Carter Smith III, *Managing Editor*
Lesley James, *Principal Writer*
Ana Deboo, *Project Editor*
Bernard Schleifer, *Art Director*
John Kern, *Cover Design*
Karen Covington, *Production Editor*

RAINTREE STECK-VAUGHN PUBLISHERS STAFF
Walter Kossmann, *Publishing Director*
Kathy DeVico, *Editor*
Max Brinkmann, *Art Director*

Photos on front cover, clockwise from top left: Pocahontas, Martha ("Calamity Jane") Cannary, Jacqueline Kennedy Onassis, Mata Hari

Photos on title page, top to bottom: Lizzie Borden, May Churchill, Iva d'Aquino, Sophie Lyons

Acknowledgments listed on page 80 constitute part of this copyright page.

Library of Congress Cataloging-in-Publication Data
James, Lesley.
    Women who made a scene: heroines, villainesses, eccentrics / Lesley James.
        p. cm.—(Remarkable women: past and present)
    Includes index.
    Summary: Brief biographies of women who were notorious for committing crimes or causing scandals, from the religious leader Aishah to the frontier heroine Betty Zane.
    ISBN 0-8172-5735-7
    1. Women—Biography—Juvenile literature. 2. Female offenders—Biography—Juvenile literature. 3. Women heroes—Biography—Juvenile literature. [1. Women—Biography. 2. Criminals. 3. Heroes. 4. Eccentrics and eccentricities.] I. Title. II. Series.
HQ1123.J36   2000
305.4'092'2—dc21
[B]   00-027236
Printed and bound in the United States
1 2 3 4 5 6 7 8 9 0 LB 03 02 01 00

CONTENTS

INTRODUCTION

WHAT DOES QUEEN MARIE-ANTOINETTE OF FRANCE HAVE IN COMMON with the American philanthropist Oseola McCarty or the Irish pirate Grace O'Malley? They—and all the other women in this book—possessed the power to fascinate. People avidly followed accounts of their exploits, gossiped about them, fell in love with them from afar or feared them, took sides and argued passionately in favor of or against them. They inspired novelists and poets and painters and musicians. Often they mystified people. Was Anna Anderson *really* the Russian princess Anastasia? (As it turns out, no.) What exactly sparked Bonnie Parker and Clyde Barrow's killing spree?

One thing is certain. Readers searching for role models in these pages should proceed with caution, always asking themselves what they think of a given woman's actions. You will find stories of remarkable courage and goodness, like those of the Nazi resistance leaders Hannah Senesh and Haviva Reik. You'll also find examples of extreme evil. By selling poison and encouraging clients to commit murder, La Toffania caused the deaths of many more people than she ever could have killed working alone. Other women in the book are strange but compelling. Florence Jenkins was known as the "world's worst opera singer," but many of her fans admired her dedication and sincerity.

There are people who strike an emotional chord with the public because of who they are, rather than what they do. Virginia Dare became the symbol of a new era by being the first baby born to English settlers in America. Then she and the other settlers of Roanoke Island disappeared, an event that still arouses speculation among history (and mystery) buffs. A real-life prince agreed with fans that actress Grace Kelly was as lovely as a fairy-tale princess, so he gave her the lifestyle to match her image. Another beauty, Evelyn Nesbit, inadvertently inspired her jealous husband to murder a man he thought was his rival. She will forever be associated with a crime she didn't commit.

Sometimes a single event catapults a person to fame. Kate Shelley saw a railroad bridge collapse and raced to the nearest station to save an oncoming train from disaster. For the rest of her life, she was a hero. Samantha Smith wrote a letter to Soviet leader Yuri Andropov, urging him to help end the Cold War. To her surprise, he answered. She became an unofficial goodwill ambassador, inspiring thousands.

One person's hero can also be another person's villain. Phoolan Devi, a bandit from a low caste in India, became a hero among other people struggling against poverty and discrimination. After being released from prison, she was elected to parliament. The case of the Mexican Indian Malintzin is especially complicated. Seeking to save local tribes from being conquered by the powerful Aztec Indians, she allied herself with Spaniard Hernán Cortés, who proceeded to conquer *all* the Indian tribes in the area. Many people consider Malintzin the worst kind of traitor. Others think of her as the mother of the *mestizos* (people of mixed European and native blood who comprise most of Mexico's population), because she and Cortés had a son.

As you read, enjoy the complexities and puzzles you encounter. Some of these women let natural emotions—anger, jealousy, greed— rule their lives. Others leapt into action in a crisis. Beatrice Cenci killed her brutal father and became a romantic heroine. We don't even know for sure if Lizzie Borden murdered her father, but the accusation ruined her reputation. Why do such contradictions occur? Is a killing ever justified? Questions like these aren't simple, but it is important to consider them. And it is proof of how fascinating these women are that their stories continue to interest and thrill us.

Photos top left Anna Anderson, bottom left Grace Kelly,
top right Evelyn Nesbit, bottom right Beatrice Cenci.

Aishah (614?–678)
Religious leader

AISHAH WAS BORN IN THE ARABIAN CITY OF Mecca, where Muhammad began teaching the values that would become the basis of the Islamic faith. In 622 Muhammad's opponents forced him to move to Medina and instigated a war with his supporters, among them Abu Bakr, who was Aishah's father and Muhammad's chief adviser. When Aishah was nine years old and Muhammad was 53, she became the third of his nine wives. Aishah was intelligent, energetic, and devoted to Muhammad and his teachings—qualities that made her his favorite wife. The war came to an end in 630, and Muhammad ruled as the supreme political and religious leader until he died two years later.

Forbidden to remarry, Aishah devoted her considerable influence to helping her father become the first Muslim caliph, or ruler. During the political turmoil that followed Abu Bakr's death, she maintained an important position, thanks to her courage and extensive learning. Her opposition to would-be caliph Ali led to civil war. Two separate Islamic branches were formed: the Sunni, who followed Aishah, and the Shia, who followed Ali. Aishah led her army into battle on camelback until she was captured by Ali in 656. He released her on condition that she stay out of leadership struggles, which she did, but her involvement in Islam remained strong. The teachings of this "Mother of the Believers" are still an important part of Islamic tradition.

Priscilla Mullins Alden (1602–?)
Colonial heroine

THE STORY OF PRISCILLA ALDEN'S MARRIAGE proposal has become part of American folklore, retold most famously in the poem, "The Courtship of Miles Standish" (1858), by Henry Wadsworth Longfellow. Priscilla set sail for Plymouth, Massachusetts, on the *Mayflower* in 1620, along with her parents, younger brother, and other Pilgrims fleeing religious persecution in their native England. During the first terrible winter at the colony, half the settlers died, including Priscilla's family. Those who survived drew close to each other and continued to work hard to survive in a harsh new land. One of the hardest working was John Alden, who fell in love with Priscilla. According to legend, so did Captain Miles Standish, his best friend. Miles asked John to woo Priscilla on his behalf, but when John asked Priscilla if she would marry Miles, Priscilla reportedly replied, "Why don't you speak for yourself, John?"

In addition to being the heroine of the first American love story, Priscilla helped the Massachusetts colony thrive, with the Aldens becoming one of its most prominent families. Her marriage to John produced 11 children, including a daughter who married Miles Standish's eldest son.

Alfhild (5th century)
Pirate

A MEDIEVAL ACCOUNT OF THE HISTORY OF THE Danes includes tales of "shield maidens," warrior women who chose to live free from men. Many of them sailed the seas during a period when piracy was, by Viking standards, a practical way to make a living rather than a crime. The most remarkable of these legendary women was Alfhild, daughter of Siward, a king of the Germanic people known as Goths.

The story goes that Alfhild put on men's clothing and became a sea rover in order to escape an unwanted marriage to a prince named Alf. With a crew of women who shared her independent attitude, she led several successful raids on Scandinavian coasts. At some point she was also elected captain of a ship whose male crew did not realize she was a woman. However, she was back on her all-women ship when Alf finally caught up with her and captured her ship in battle. Back in women's clothes, Alfhild married Alf, her seafaring days at an end.

Anna Anderson (1901?–1984)
Impostor

IN 1920 POLICE RESCUED A WOMAN WHO HAD jumped into an icy canal in Berlin, Germany. She claimed to have no memory of her identity. While recovering in a mental hospital, she read a magazine article about the 1918 assassination of Czar Nicholas II of Russia and his family by

Mary Baker (Princess Caraboo) (1800?–?)
Impostor

IN APRIL 1817 AN EXOTICALLY DRESSED YOUNG woman appeared in the village of Almondsbury in Gloucestershire, England. She conveyed through sign language that she needed food and shelter and gave no indication of understanding English. The magistrate of the county, Mr. Worrall, and his wife took her in, even though Mrs. Worrall suspected that the mysterious stranger was an impostor. She didn't have the heart to evict the girl, who identified herself as "Caraboo."

Caraboo spoke and wrote in a "foreign" language, which scholars tried unsuccessfully to place. She also climbed trees, shot arrows, played a tambourine, and engaged in other non-English activities. Scholars came to study her, and she was treated as a celebrity, especially after a Portuguese sailor appeared who could "interpret" her language. Then she was able to reveal that she was a princess from an Indonesian island, who had been kidnapped by pirates and had escaped from their ship off the shore of England.

Caraboo's celebrity lasted only a year before she was recognized by someone who had known her as Mary Baker, a Devonshire servant girl with a wild imagination and a passion for play-acting. The "sailor" had been in on the scheme from the beginning. Kindly Mrs. Worrall paid for her passage to America, and Baker was never heard from again.

Bolshevik revolutionary soldiers. The article suggested that one of the Czar's daughters, Anastasia, had survived. Suddenly, the unknown woman announced that she was that princess, saved from the massacre by loyal soldiers.

Because of her remarkable resemblance to Anastasia, which included unique scars, and because tests such as handwriting analysis identified her as the princess, many people believed her story. Some royal family members supported her lawsuit to claim the Romanov inheritance and were impressed by her recollections of life in prerevolutionary Russia. Others doubted her, pointing out that she couldn't speak Russian. Even so, her story caught the world's imagination because she represented hope in a war-torn time and because of the strength of her belief.

The woman spent much of her life in hospitals, suffering from depression, and went by the name Anna Anderson to protect her privacy. She spent her last years with her American husband, John Manahan, in Charlottesville, Virginia. In September 1994, ten years after her death, the skeletons in the Romanovs' grave were identified, including that of Anastasia. One month later, tests comparing Anderson's DNA to that of the Romanov family proved conclusively that she was not Anastasia but very likely Franziska Schanzkowski, a poor Polish farm girl.

Kate "Ma" Barker (1872?–1935)
Outlaw, gang leader

FROM AN EARLY AGE, KATE CLARK ADMIRED fellow Missouri-born outlaws Frank and Jesse James and was determined to have a gang just like theirs. After she married George Barker, a poor sharecropper, she gave birth to four sons, Herman, Lloyd, Arthur, and Fred, who began getting arrested for petty crimes before they were even in their teens. Barker always attended the trials and pleaded eloquently in defense of her boys, who were both dominated and adored by their "Ma." By 1927 she had left her husband behind and embarked on a life of crime that included kidnappings and numerous

robberies of post offices and banks throughout the Midwest.

Barker was never arrested or charged with a crime. She stayed in the background as the "brains" of the gang, planning the heists that her sons and other criminals carried out. After Herman was killed in a confrontation with a policeman, she unleashed a series of violent crimes that made her the Federal Bureau of Investigation's (FBI) Public Enemy Number One. FBI chief J. Edgar Hoover called her "a veritable beast of prey." In 1935 FBI agents tracked Barker down at a Florida resort where she was hiding with Freddie after attempting to disguise her identity by having her fingerprints removed. She and Freddie were killed in a gun battle. Arthur and Lloyd also came to violent ends.

Helena Petrovna Blavatsky (1831–1891)
Mystic, writer

HELENA HAHN WAS BORN IN THE UKRAINE TO A Russian military officer and his wife, a novelist and women's rights advocate. Young Helena was a hypnotizing storyteller who surrounded herself with mystery and fantasy. For a few months at age 17, she was married to the much older General Nikifor

Blavatsky. Leaving him to travel the world, she experienced perilous adventures and discovered her interest in the spiritual traditions of the East.

In 1873—having become "Madame Blavatsky"—she settled in New York City and began a writing and journal-editing career. With H. S. Olcott, she founded the Theosophical Society to promote her idea that a "universal brotherhood of man" could be attained through the study of ancient philosophical and religious systems. The society attracted many followers, mostly due to the "miracles" that Blavatsky performed and the psychic powers she claimed to possess. These included clairvoyance and the ability to channel the spirits of ancient wise men. In 1879 Blavatsky established a theosophical headquarters in India. When the London Society for Psychical Research sent a representative, Richard Hodgson, to investigate her organization, he concluded that she was a fake.

> "All things that ever were, that are, or that will be, have their record upon the astral light, or tablet of the unseen universe; the initiated adept, by using the vision of his own spirit, can know all that has been known or can be known."
>
> HELENA BLAVATSKY
> *Isis Unveiled*

Blavatsky returned to Europe in the late 1880s. Although she suffered throughout her adult life from poor health and accusations of fraud, she had over 100,000 followers at the time of her death. Her works, including the books *Isis Unveiled* (1877) and *The Secret Doctrine* (1888), continue to inspire people to this day.

Gertrudis Bocanegra (1765–1817)
Patriot

WOMEN PLAYED IMPORTANT ROLES IN THE Mexican War of Independence. One of the most notable was Gertrudis Bocanegra, who was 45 years old when the freedom fighter and priest Father Miguel Hidalgo called on Mexican patriots to take up arms against Spain. Most of the rebels were poor

Indians or *mestizos* (people of mixed heritage) who wanted economic and social reform. Others, such as Gertrudis, were upper-class Creoles (people born in the New World to Spanish parents) who wanted to replace the monarchy with a republic. Before the war Gertrudis had organized schools for Indian children. Now she organized an underground army of women, including herself and her daughters. She urged her husband, who had been an officer in the royal army, to join the rebels. With her young son in tow, she gathered information and supplies and carried messages between rebel groups.

After eight years Gertrudis's husband, her son, and Father Hidalgo had all been killed. She was sent as a spy to her hometown of Pátzcuaro, where she was recognized and arrested. The Spanish government tortured her to gain information about her compatriots. When she refused to betray them, she was publicly executed by a firing squad. Gertrudis's sacrifices were justified when Mexico gained its independence in 1821.

Anne Bonny (1697?–?)

Mary Read (1690s?–1721)
Pirates

IN OCTOBER 1720 A PIRATE SHIP WAS CAPTURED by the British governor's men off the coast of Jamaica. Only two of the pirates fought courageously; the rest hid below decks. Those two were Anne Bonny and Mary Read.

The illegitimate daughter of a serving woman, Anne had been born in County Cork, Ireland. The scandal of her birth forced her wealthy father to flee with his family to America, where she grew up on his Carolina plantation. Anne married a sailor named James Bonny, who tried to steal her father's fortune, causing her to be disinherited. Before long, she had left her husband for Calico Jack Rackham, one of the most notorious pirates of the Caribbean. Wearing men's clothing and expertly wielding pistol and sword, Anne became as feared as Calico Jack, even commanding the ship when he was too drunk to do so.

One of the sailors captured by Calico Jack who chose to become a pirate rather than "walk the plank" was Mary Read—although only Anne knew she was a woman. The two became fast friends. Mary, a native

Anne Bonny

of Devon, England, had been disguised and raised as a boy so she could inherit from her father's family. Enjoying the freedom offered by her disguise, Mary joined the army in Flanders (now a part of Belgium). She returned to dresses to marry a fellow soldier and run a tavern, but after her husband's death, she went back to trousers and the fighting life, this time at sea.

After their capture in 1720, Calico Jack and his crew were hanged, except for Anne and Mary, who claimed they were pregnant to escape execution. Mary died of fever in prison, but Anne was released and never heard of again.

Lizzie Borden (1860–1927)
Accused murderer

LIZZIE BORDEN WAS KNOWN TO THE TOWNSPEOPLE of Fall River, Massachusetts, as a gentle Sunday school teacher. Her mother had died when she was two years old, and her father, a wealthy but stern and stingy man, had remarried three years later. Lizzie and her older sister, Emma, were constantly at odds with their father and stepmother, mostly over money.

On August 4, 1892, while Emma was away on a visit, Mr. Borden went out, leaving his wife, Lizzie, and the maid at home. He returned home to take a nap. At about 11:15 A.M., Lizzie woke the maid to tell her that she had just come in from the barn and found her father dead. He had been hit on the head with a sharp instrument. Mrs. Borden's body was found upstairs, also mutilated, and examination showed that she had died about an hour before her husband.

All the evidence pointed toward Lizzie, but she wouldn't confess, even after being held in jail for almost a year. Neither witnesses nor a murder weapon could be found. In June 1893 Lizzie's 13-day trial fascinated the nation, which was split on the question of her guilt. The jury was unanimous, though, and acquitted her after an hour's deliberation. Lizzie inherited her father's wealth and continued to live in Fall River as a social outcast until her death.

Lucrezia Borgia (1480–1519)
Noblewoman

LUCREZIA BORGIA WAS CONSIDERED ONE OF THE most beautiful, and most wicked, women of the Italian Renaissance. She might have been a poisoner like her notorious father and brother—or she might have been an unwilling participant in their intrigues and treachery.

Lucrezia, born to the powerful Rodrigo Borgia and his mistress, was raised with Rodrigo's other illegitimate children. Charming and talented, she was married at age 13 to Giovanni Sforza, a political ally of her father's. When Rodrigo (who had by then been elected Pope Alexander VI) changed alliances, Giovanni became one of the Borgias' many enemies. The marriage was annulled, and in 1498 Lucrezia wed Alfonso, Duke of Bisceglie. Although Lucrezia tried to protect him, Alfonso was murdered two years later by her brother Cesare. Many of her lovers were killed by Cesare, who wanted to come first in his sister's affections. Lucrezia was often accused of having played a part in the crimes he planned.

Determined to escape her family's control, Lucrezia chose her third husband, Alfonso d'Este, Duke of Ferrara. Her father died in 1503, accidentally poisoned by Cesare, who was forced into exile when a Borgia enemy was elected pope. Lucrezia was finally free. The arts flourished at Ferrara under her patronage (she herself had studied with painter Leonardo da Vinci). When she died, she was mourned as a devout wife and mother.

Cordelia Botkin (1854?–1910)
Poisoner

CORDELIA BOTKIN WAS A BORED HOUSEWIFE. John Dunning was a respected, and married, journalist. The two shared a passion for the wild life of San Francisco in the 1890s—and for each other. During their affair, Mrs. Dunning waited patiently for her husband to come to his senses, even after he lost his job and began living on the money Cordelia received from her own husband.

In 1898 Dunning was hired by the Associated Press to cover the Spanish American War and left town, hinting to Cordelia that he missed his wife. Not long afterward, Mrs. Dunning received a box of chocolates in the mail. She shared the candy with her sister, and both women died of arsenic poisoning. Mr. Dunning identified the handwriting on the enclosed note as Cordelia's. Other evidence was also found that convicted her.

Sentenced to life imprisonment, Cordelia charmed her jailers into allowing her a luxuriously furnished cell, meals from restaurants, and shopping sprees in town. After the 1906 earthquake ruined the county jail, she was moved to San Quentin, where she died.

Belle Boyd (1844–1900)
Confederate spy

BELLE BOYD PERFORMED HER FIRST SERVICE FOR the Confederate army when she was still a teenager. It was 1861, and Union forces had occupied her hometown of Martinsburg, West Virginia. A drunken soldier tried to force his way into her house to raise the Union flag. Seventeen-year-old Belle shot and killed him, but she was acquitted of murder by a sympathetic jury.

Belle became a spy for the generals P. G. T. Beauregard and Thomas J. "Stonewall" Jackson. She was arrested several times but always released, because her captors considered her "too charming to be a spy." In her most daring escapade—crossing enemy lines while bullets flew close enough around her to tear holes in her skirt—she brought information that helped win the battle of Front Royal for the South in 1862.

In 1864 Boyd was on her way to England to deliver letters for Confederate president Jefferson Davis, when her ship was captured. The Union captain in charge, Samuel Hardinge, fell in love with her and allowed her to escape. As punishment, Hardinge was discharged from service. Free to follow Boyd to England, he married her. After his death the following year, Belle made her living first as an actress in England and America, then as a traveling lecturer, thrilling audiences with tales of her exploits.

Eva Braun (1912–1945)
Mistress of Adolf Hitler

IN 1929 EVA BRAUN WAS WORKING AS AN ASSISTANT to Heinrich Hoffmann, the official photographer for Adolf Hitler, then an aspiring politician. Within three years the future Führer of Germany and the attractive young woman had begun a romantic relationship. Hitler bought Eva a villa, and eventually she moved into his Alpine chalet in Berchtesgaden. Braun loved to swim, ski, and read romance novels; she had no interest at all in politics. Her consuming passion was Hitler himself, although she often wrote in her diaries that he neglected and mistreated her. She was his companion throughout World War II but was never allowed to be seen with him in public.

During the last days of the war, with the Russians closing in on Berlin, Eva joined Hitler in his bunker. She refused to leave, despite his orders, and

Adolf Hitler with Eva Braun

proclaimed her undying loyalty to him. It's believed that they were married in a civil ceremony just before midnight on April 29, 1945. Only a few hours later, the newlyweds committed suicide by taking poison, and their bodies were cremated by loyal soldiers.

Marie, Marquise de Brinvilliers (1630?–1676)
Poisoner

MARIE DE BRINVILLIERS, ALTHOUGH WEALTHY, needed even more money for the extravagances of life at King Louis XIV's court in France. She also wanted to punish her father, the head of the Paris police, for having her lover, Gaudin de Sainte-Croix, imprisoned in the Bastille. She solved both problems in 1666 by poisoning her father and inheriting part of the family fortune. She proceeded to poison her two brothers—and anyone else who got in her way. Her husband, Antoine Gobelin de Brinvilliers, would have become one of her victims, if Sainte-Croix (who had no desire to marry her) had not continually administered antidotes to him.

Marie tested poisons on her servants and on hundreds of patients at the public hospital where she paid "charitable" visits. Authorities were suspicious but could prove nothing. Then, in 1672, Sainte-Croix died after accidentally inhaling a poison he was concocting, and evidence in his papers revealed the murders. Marie fled abroad, but she was eventually found in a convent in Liège, Belgium. She was brought back to Paris, tried, and executed. Although she had refused to reveal the names of any fellow poisoners, even under torture, her conviction started a police round-up of hundreds, including the notorious La Voisin, in what became known as the "Affair of the Poisons."

Margaret Tobin Brown (1867–1932)
Popular heroine

THE WOMAN WHOSE STORY INSPIRED THE STAGE and film musical *The Unsinkable Molly Brown* (1960, 1964) started life as Maggie Tobin in Hannibal, Missouri. There the impoverished young girl met writer Samuel Clemens (Mark Twain), a

Molly's Tall Tales

There are many colorful tales about Molly Brown. One is about the time J. J. Brown brought home money for his mining payroll. Molly put it in the stove for safekeeping but forgot to tell her husband. That night, a chill was in the air, so J. J. lit the stove, sending their money up in flames. They burned about $75, but Molly liked to claim that they had lost a "fortune" of $300,000. Her adventures often grew more bizarre with each telling, because she loved a good story and couldn't help tinkering with the truth.

frequent diner at the restaurant where she worked. He advised her to head West for the gold rush, which she did in 1884. In the mining town of Leadville, Colorado, she met and married J. J. Brown, who soon struck gold. To Maggie's disappointment, the *nouveau riche* Browns were considered too unsophisticated to gain acceptance in Denver society. She kept trying, though, and eventually found her way into the parties of the rich and famous as a high-spirited storyteller. Although her husband left her, he continued to support her financially until his death.

Brown's unladylike manner came in handy in 1912, when she found herself onboard the sinking luxury ship *Titanic*. She bullied the women in her lifeboat into rowing to safety, supposedly pulling the oars for seven hours herself, and then tirelessly nursed survivors on the rescue ship. She delighted in the exaggerated stories that turned her into a legend, but, despite her celebrity, she died in genteel poverty in New York City.

Lady Eleanor Butler (1739–1829)

Sarah Ponsonby (1755–1831)
The "Ladies of Llangollen"

IN 1778 LADY ELEANOR BUTLER AND SARAH Ponsonby shocked their families by disguising themselves in men's clothing and running away together. That first attempt at setting up a shared life was unsuccessful; they were caught and brought back home. Sarah's family was a prosperous one living in Dublin. Eleanor belonged to the Irish aristocracy; her childhood home was a castle in Kilkenny, and she had been educated at a convent school in France. The two women had met when Sarah was 13 and Eleanor was 29. Their friendship flourished based on their shared interests, which did not include traditional marriage.

The next time Eleanor and Sarah tried to set up a household together, in 1780, they not only succeeded but convinced their families to grant them small incomes. They settled in a cottage called Plas Newydd in Llangollen, Wales, and left home so infrequently that it was rumored they spent every night there for the next 50 years.

Lady Eleanor Butler and Sarah Ponsonby

The "Ladies of Llangollen" became objects of great curiosity to a society unused to two women living together in romantic friendship. Their intention was to remain in seclusion, dedicating themselves to reading and scholarly pursuits. However, many famous people, among them the writers William Wordsworth and Sir Walter Scott, came to visit the ladies and made them the subject of poems and other literary works. They were especially known for communing with nature in their garden, which they tended devotedly.

Mary Peck Butterworth (1686–1775)
Counterfeiter

IN 1716 MARY BUTTERWORTH SET UP A SMALL business in her kitchen in Rehoboth, Massachusetts, then part of the Plymouth Colony. Unlike her neighbors with home enterprises like spinning or candle-making, Butterworth produced counterfeit money. At first she was assisted by her husband, John, and other relatives. Eventually the business employed several prominent townspeople, including a judge. Butterworth perfected a system of reproducing bills that did not require printing them from engraved copper plates, which were hard to destroy and provided incriminating evidence. She transferred a genuine bill's image onto a piece of starched muslin using a hot iron and then pressed the muslin against a blank piece of paper. The details were filled in with a quill pen and ink.

By 1723 the authorities had grown suspicious. A member of Butterworth's group confessed to the crime, leading to the arrest of Butterworth and several of her accomplices. However, there was no physical evidence for their accusers to use against them, since the pieces of muslin had been destroyed. Butterworth was released and retired to the life of a respectable housewife.

Henriette Rainouard Caillaux (1877–1943)
Assassin, socialite

THE YEAR 1913 FOUND FRANCE ON THE BRINK of war with Germany and suffering from internal turmoil. In Paris the right-wing conservative Gaston Calmette used his position as editor of the newspaper *Le Figaro* to launch attacks on the left-leaning minister of finance, Joseph Caillaux. Calmette called the politician a liar, thief, and secret ally of the Germans. When he went so far as to publish the finance minister's private love letters, Caillaux's wife, Henriette, who had been growing increasingly angry at the editor's tactics, finally snapped.

On March 16, 1914, Henriette went to Calmette's office and shot him to death at his desk. She calmly gave herself up, declaring that the only justice in

France was the revolver, and awaited her trial in St. Lazare Prison, dining on meals from expensive restaurants. Her sensational trial, in which politics mixed with high society scandal, obsessed the country. Even the outbreak of World War I didn't push it off the front pages of the papers. Eventually the jury acquitted Henriette on the grounds that, as a member of the "emotional sex," she was not responsible for her crime of passion. Even so, the murder finished what Calmette had started: As a result of the scandal, Caillaux resigned his office. The couple left France for several years, and although Joseph did later resume his political career, he never again held such power.

Jeanne Calment (1875–1997)
Oldest known person

DURING THE 1990S THE ENTIRE POPULATION OF Arles, France, celebrated each February 21. This was the birthday of one of the town's most beloved inhabitants, Jeanne Calment, the longest-living person whose birth date could be verified. Calment was born the year the Eiffel Tower was built in Paris and once met the painter Vincent Van Gogh. She married at age 21 but outlived her husband, daughter, and grandson. When she was 90 years old, a lawyer offered to pay her a monthly income if he could have her apartment when she died. He ended up spending more than double the property's value— and he never got to move in. He died the year before she did.

> "I waited 110 years to be famous. I intend to make the most of it for as long as possible."
> JEANNE CALMENT,
> after reaching the age of 110

Calment credited her long life to her consumption of lots of olive oil and judicious amounts of wine. She also enjoyed music and sports and had a wry sense of humor. She took up fencing at age 85 and rode a bicycle until she was 100. At age 121 she recorded her memoirs, *Time's Mistress*, and released them on compact disc. Although blind, hard of hearing, and confined to a wheelchair at the end, she was still full of witticisms and declared she had never been bored.

Martha "Calamity Jane" Cannary (1852–1903)
Frontierswoman

CALAMITY JANE'S STORY HAS BEEN SO DISTORTED by her own tall tales and by the exaggerations of journalists eager to portray her as a "typical" Wild West character that it's hard to tell truth from fiction. It is generally known that she headed West on a wagon train in the 1860s and was orphaned at an early age. Always a wandering spirit, she moved often, earning her living however she could, sometimes as a prostitute. She ended up in the gold mining town of Deadwood, South Dakota, in 1876. There is evidence that she worked as a bull whacker, driving ox teams across the plains, that she helped nurse miners stricken with smallpox, and that she met the legendary frontiersman Wild Bill Hickok. But— despite her claims—there is no evidence that she and Hickok got married and had a child, that she ever fought Indians, or that she rode for the Pony Express.

Calamity Jane demanded equal rights and respect, something few women insisted on in that era. She wore men's clothes, joined in saloon brawls, and was often arrested for howling, cursing, and firing guns while drunk. She came to

national attention as a star of Buffalo Bill's Wild West Show and other exhibitions that romanticized frontier life. She died of pneumonia near Deadwood and was buried, by her request, next to Hickok.

Elizabeth Canning (1734–1773)
Perjurer

IN EARLY 1753 ALL OF ENGLAND WAS FASCINATED by a trial taking place in London. Half the country supported 18-year-old Elizabeth Canning, a servant girl who claimed she had been abducted by an old gypsy woman and her gang of outlaws. The other half rallied around the old woman, Mary Squires, who could produce dozens of witnesses to swear she had been miles away from London at the time. After hearing Canning's story of how she had been kept locked up without food or water for four weeks, the court condemned Squires to death. Another old woman, "Mother" Wells, was convicted when Canning identified her house as the site of her imprisonment. The girl's statements varied widely each time she gave them, but she had a good reputation and an innocent manner, while the public was repelled by the unsavory looks of the old gypsies.

In the end the Lord Mayor of London stepped in and insured the acquittal of Squires and Wells. Canning was then tried for perjury, found guilty, and transported to America, where she is believed to have married a Quaker and become a schoolteacher. She never revealed where she spent those weeks of her "abduction," why her clothes were in tatters when she returned, or why she had concocted such a sensational tale.

Lucretia ("Patty") Cannon (1783?–1829)
Gang leader, murderer

PATTY CANNON'S TAVERN, AT A CROSSROADS ON the Maryland-Delaware border, was a popular place for traveling businessmen to stop for a bite to eat and a bed for the night. Mrs. Cannon was a generous hostess whose bills were low—unless you were traveling with lots of money or slaves. In that case the innkeeper (or one of her brutal assistants) would kill you, take your money, and sell your slaves. Cannon eventually confessed to murdering at least 11 people herself and directing her gang to murder more than a dozen others. She was also responsible for kidnapping free black people and selling them into slavery. Those who were too young or too old, she cruelly disposed of.

A large, strong woman, Patty Hanly was born near Montreal, Canada. She married Alonzo Cannon at age 16, but he died three years later of what turned out to be poison administered by his wife. For the next 27 years, Patty planned and executed crimes with the help of her gang. At last Cannon's neighbors grew suspicious, and she was arrested. She was sentenced to death but committed suicide before the sentence could be carried out.

Margaret Catchpole (1762–1819)
Daredevil

MARGARET CATCHPOLE FIRST SHOWED HER unbeatable courage at age 13 by making a daring bareback ride to fetch emergency medical help. She eventually became a servant in the house of John Cobbold of Ipswich, England, and saved one of his children from drowning. However, while her refusal to let any obstacle stand in her way made her a heroine, it also made her a criminal. In 1797, determined to join the man she loved, she disguised herself as a sailor, stole Cobbold's horse, and rode to London at breakneck speed. She was captured and condemned to death for horse stealing, but then the sentence was changed to exile in Australia. Before she could be sent, the dauntless Catchpole broke out of jail, but she was recaptured and deported in 1801.

A new life began for Catchpole in the Australian colony, where she worked as a housekeeper and property overseer. She recorded vivid accounts of her experiences in her letters to relatives and her former master's family. These letters inspired a book by Richard Cobbold, John's son, but much of Catchpole's true story was lost in the loose adaptation. She was pardoned in 1814 and chose to remain in Australia. There she ran a store and worked as a midwife and nurse, eventually dying of influenza contracted from one of her patients.

Edith Cavell (1865–1915)
Nurse, war heroine

EDITH CAVELL'S FATHER, AN ENGLISH CLERGYMAN, taught his serious-minded daughter to hold the virtues of duty and sacrifice above all others. After caring for her father during an illness in 1895, she chose to devote herself to nursing and was trained at the London Hospital. In 1907 Cavell was invited to become the matron of the Berkendael Institute in Brussels, a new nurses' training school. Under her strict discipline, the school was a success, and Cavell chose to remain there after World War I began in 1914.

The career that would make her a heroine began that year, when two wounded British soldiers were brought in, having narrowly escaped from behind enemy lines. She helped them to return to England and soon found herself part of an underground network helping other fugitive soldiers and men of military age to escape the Germans and join the Allied forces. Cavell provided not only refuge and medical care, but money, identification papers, and guides. Often she led soldiers to meeting places herself, aiding over 200 British, French, and Belgian men.

Cavell's nursing school had been converted into a Red Cross hospital by the Germans, who became suspicious of the matron's actions, although she nursed both the Allied and the enemy soldiers with equal care. In 1915 Cavell was arrested, tried, and executed by a firing squad, to the outrage of the Allied nations.

Beatrice Cenci (1577–1599)
Murderer, literary heroine

ALTHOUGH 16TH-CENTURY ROME WAS FILLED with corrupt characters, Francesco Cenci was notorious for his viciousness. Because he was also a wealthy and powerful nobleman, his cruelty went unchecked. Francesco took his daughter, Beatrice, and her stepmother, Lucrezia, away from Rome and imprisoned them in the isolated castle of La Petrella. Beatrice found comfort with the castle steward, Olimpio Calvetti. With the help of Olimpio and her brother Giacomo, she plotted to murder her monstrous father.

On September 9, 1598, Francesco tumbled from a balcony in what his family claimed was an accident. It was soon revealed that he had been dead at the time of the fall and that a hired assassin had been involved. The entire Cenci family was arrested and tortured until they confessed to their parts in the crime. The public felt great sympathy for the accused, but Pope Clement VIII refused to grant them mercy. Beatrice, Giacomo, and Lucrezia were beheaded, and their property was confiscated by the pope, who may have

> "Farewell, my tender brother. Think
> of our sad fate with gentleness, as now:
> And let mild, pitying thoughts lighten for thee
> Thy sorrow's load. . . .
>   **And tho'**
> Ill tongues shall wound me, and our common
>   name
> Be as a mark stamped on thine innocent brow
> For men to point at as they pass, do thou
> Forbear, and never think a thought unkind
> Of those, who perhaps love thee in their
>   graves."
>
> **speech by Beatrice in *The Cenci*,
> by PERCY BYSSHE SHELLEY**

withheld pardon in order to gain the lands. The fate of Beatrice and her family has inspired artwork, poetry, novels, and plays, including the verse tragedy *The Cenci* (1819), by Percy Bysshe Shelley.

Elizabeth "Cassie" Chadwick (1857–1907)
Impostor, confidence artist

DURING THE 1890S CASSIE CHADWICK, A GENTEEL doctor's wife from Cleveland, Ohio, paid a visit to New York City, where she asked a gossipy acquaintance to accompany her to the house of the famously wealthy steel magnate Andrew Carnegie. The friend waited in the carriage, full of curiosity, while Chadwick was inside. When she returned from the "visit," she "accidentally" dropped a note, apparently signed by Carnegie, promising to pay her several hundred thousand dollars. On questioning, Chadwick said that she was Carnegie's illegitimate daughter. She begged her friend to keep the secret, but the news spread like wildfire. When banks learned of her prospects, they offered to loan her illegally large sums of money at high interest rates.

Chadwick lived lavishly, borrowing more money from banks and individuals to pay back the interest from earlier loans, until in 1904 a Boston bank noticed her enormous debts and refused to give her a loan. Suddenly all her creditors wanted to be paid, but the money had been spent. It was revealed that Chadwick was actually the daughter of a poor Canadian farmer and that she had made her living by fraud, blackmail, and prostitution before her marriage. No one had dared to ask the unmarried Carnegie if he had a child, nor did anyone believe that a woman would have the intelligence and daring to pull off such a swindle. Chadwick was put in prison, where she died three years later.

Alice Lynne Chamberlain (1948–)
Murder suspect

IN AUGUST 1980 LINDY CHAMBERLAIN, A 32-YEAR-old Australian woman, drove to Uluru (also called Ayers Rock) for a camping trip with her husband, the pastor of a Seventh Day Adventist church, their two sons, and their two-month-old daughter, Azaria. The second evening of the trip, Azaria disappeared. At the inquest Chamberlain explained that, while making dinner over the campfire, she heard the baby cry, saw a dingo (a kind of wild dog) run out of the tent with something in its mouth, and discovered that the baby was gone. The family roused a search party, but only some torn, bloodstained clothing was found. The authorities believed her account.

However, one forensic scientist was not convinced that the bloodstains and holes were caused by a dingo, and the case was reopened. The sensational press reports created a flurry of public interest and debate over Chamberlain's possible guilt. In 1982 Chamberlain, by then pregnant with her fourth child, was sentenced to life imprisonment. Her husband was given a suspended sentence as an accessory.

In 1986 Azaria's jacket was discovered at the base of Ayers Rock, leading to further investigation and ultimately overturning the evidence that had convicted Chamberlain. She was released from prison and given $1.3 million in compensation for her ordeal.

Ch'ing Yih Szaou (1775–1844)
Pirate

ONE OF THE MOST FAMOUS CHINESE PIRATES WAS a woman, Lady Ch'ing Yih Szaou (also known as Ching Hsi Kai). She may have been born into a pirate clan and grown up on a boat, learning the family trade. When her husband was killed in 1807, she assumed his position as leader of a floating nation of around 50,000 people. She controlled the seas south of China, offering safe passage for a fee and seizing cargoes and hostages from those who wouldn't pay. She also raided estates on the coast belonging to wealthy mandarins, or public officials, but was sympathetic to the poorer inhabitants. It is said that she forbade her people to harm peasants and required that women be treated with respect.

For years the Chinese, Portuguese, and English tried to destroy the powerful pirate queen without success. At last the Chinese navy managed to cripple, though not destroy, her fleet. The government also kept ships from her waters, starving her of her prey, so that she began plundering the peasant villages she had formerly protected. Lady Ch'ing accepted an offer of amnesty in 1810 and was not only pardoned but given an income and a high place in society, which enabled her to set up shop as a smuggler.

May Churchill (1876–1929)
Swindler

Mᴀʏ Cʜᴜʀᴄʜɪʟʟ ᴡᴀꜱ ʙᴏʀɴ ɪɴ Iʀᴇʟᴀɴᴅ, ʙᴜᴛ ꜱʜᴇ became known as "Chicago May," after the city where she rose to the height of her profession. Because of her startling beauty, she didn't need to trick men out of money, but she enjoyed the danger of the con game. She was especially known for luring men into compromising situations and then blackmailing them. Often arrested, she escaped serious punishment every time, amassed a fortune, and ruined men in the United States, Europe, and South America.

May's downfall was a notorious jewel thief, Eddie Guerin, with whom she began a tempestuous affair in 1901. Together with two accomplices, they robbed the American Express Company offices in Paris. Churchill initially escaped arrest but was caught when she went to visit Guerin in jail to make sure he hadn't implicated her. She served three years in a French prison. Guerin

escaped from the remote penal colony where he'd been imprisoned, but the couple's reunion in England was far from harmonious. They fought bitterly, and Churchill persuaded someone to shoot Guerin, who was wounded. Once again, she was arrested. After serving 12 years for attempted murder, she was deported to America. Churchill later wrote in her memoirs, *Chicago May: Her Story* (1928), that she had no regrets about her life of crime.

Lillie Hitchcock Coit (1843–1929)
Firefighter

Lɪʟʟɪᴇ Hɪᴛᴄʜᴄᴏᴄᴋ'ꜱ ꜰᴀᴍɪʟʏ ᴍᴏᴠᴇᴅ ᴛᴏ Sᴀɴ Francisco, California, when she was ten years old. From the moment she saw the men of Knickerbocker Engine Company No. 5 in action, she became obsessed with firefighters. She was so often to be found helping fight fires that she became an honorary member of the Knickerbocker No. 5. She gained a reputation for spending all her time with the volunteers, joining them in smoking cigars, drinking bourbon, and playing poker. She even wore men's clothes and a fireman's hat to elegant dinners and had the No. 5 emblem embroidered on her underclothes.

Engaged more than a dozen times before she turned 20, Lillie finally married Howard Coit, a wealthy older man. During the wedding rehearsal, she heard her beloved engine company going by and rushed to help, ruining her wedding dress. After her marriage Lillie lived at the Palace Hotel while in the city, on an estate in Napa County, or abroad. Ironically, she was in Paris during the disastrous fire that followed the San Francisco earthquake of 1906. Upon her death she left her money to the city, specifying that it be used for beautification and to erect a memorial to the firefighters. The famous Coit Tower stands on top of Telegraph Hill.

Janet Cooke (1954–)
Author of false newspaper story

Oɴ Sᴇᴘᴛᴇᴍʙᴇʀ 28, 1980, ᴛʜᴇ Wᴀꜱʜɪɴɢᴛᴏɴ Pᴏꜱᴛ published an article by reporter Janet Cooke entitled "Jimmy's World." The story of an eight-year-old heroin addict inspired an emotional response from the public and won Janet the prestigious Pulitzer Prize the following year. Just two days after the award was announced, however, it was revealed that "Jimmy" didn't exist. The story was a work of fiction.

There had been doubts about Cooke's article all along: She discouraged another reporter from visiting Jimmy and refused to reveal her sources, claiming her life would be in danger if she did so. But the final straw was the revelation that she had lied on her résumé. Among other credentials, she listed herself as an honors graduate of Vassar College, the recipient of a master's degree in journalism from the University of Toledo, and a member of the National Association of Black Journalists.

In truth Cooke had spent only her freshman year at Vassar. She had earned only a bachelor's degree from the university in Toledo, Ohio, her hometown. She finally confessed her deception, returned the Pulitzer, and resigned from the *Post*, which reported on its own investigation of the hoax and thus maintained its reputation.

Charlotte Corday (1768–1793)
Assassin, patriot

IN JULY 1793 A 24-YEAR-OLD WOMAN FROM AN impoverished noble family set out to walk the 200 miles (322 km) from Normandy to Paris. Her name was Marie-Anne-Charlotte Corday d'Armont, and she intended to "save France." This was at the height of the Reign of Terror following the French Revolution, during which the radical revolutionaries, the Jacobins, crushed the more moderate revolutionaries, the Girondists. Corday's hometown of Caen had become a center for the Girondists, and they greatly influenced Corday, who already sympathized with the overthrown royal family. She planned to prevent further bloodshed by assassinating Jean-Paul Marat, a powerful politician whose influential newspaper, *L'ami du peuple* (The friend of the people), urged readers to kill anyone who stood in the way of the revolution.

Corday gained admittance to Marat's house by pretending that she had information to give him about a Girondist conspiracy. Marat received her while sitting in the medicinal bathtub where he spent most of his time because of a skin disease.

Charlotte Corday is captured after assassinating Marat.

While Marat made notes about the nonexistent dissidents, Corday drew out a large knife that she had hidden in her dress and stabbed him to death. She was captured, brought to trial, and sent to the guillotine in the Place de la Révolution (today the Place de la Concorde). Many Girondists were punished as a result of the assassination.

Cheryl Crane (1944–)
Homicide

AS THE ONLY CHILD OF MOVIE STAR LANA TURNER, Cheryl Crane grew up in the luxury of Beverly Hills. She adored her famous mother, but because Turner was so busy, they rarely spent much time together. Turner also had a knack for becoming involved with the wrong men. On the night of April 4, 1958, Turner, who had been divorced four times, was in the midst of a violent argument with her latest boyfriend, gangster John Stompanato. Fourteen-year-old Cheryl burst into the room, and minutes later Stompanato was lying dead on the floor with a butcher's knife in his stomach. The girl was jailed and charged first with murder, then the lesser crime of manslaughter. Turner begged to take the blame

Cheryl Crane (right) with her mother, Lana Turner

herself—and later rumors circulated in Hollywood that she really had killed Stompanato. At Crane's trial Turner's emotional testimony so moved the jury at the coroner's inquest that they returned a verdict of justifiable homicide.

After the inquest, Crane was released into the custody of her grandmother, but she ran away so often that she was placed in a reform school and later spent time in a mental institution. Eventually she discovered that she possessed exceptional business skills. She worked for her father, restaurateur Stephen Crane, and then found success as a real estate broker in San Francisco.

Caresse Crosby (1892–1970)
Socialite, publisher

THROUGHOUT HER LIFE POLLY JACOB DEVOTED her boundless energy and creativity to a remarkable variety of endeavors, beginning in 1913, when she invented the bra. Tired of wearing uncomfortable corsets, she came up with the "backless brassiere," and even took out a patent. This was shocking behavior for a wealthy New York City debutante. She married Boston banker Richard

Peabody in 1915 but left him and their two children seven years later to marry fellow socialite Harry Crosby. The Crosbys moved to Paris, where Polly changed her name to Caresse, and proceeded to live a life of flamboyant eccentricity. One of Caresse's many escapades was riding naked on a baby elephant down the Champs-Élysées.

The guests at the Crosbys' wild parties included some of the greatest writers and artists of the day. In 1927 the couple started the Black Sun Press, mainly as a means for publishing their own mediocre poetry. They soon became known for their skillful publication of works by such literary luminaries as James Joyce and D. H. Lawrence. Harry, whose mental health had deteriorated, committed suicide in 1929. Caresse went on to produce affordable paperback editions and a respected journal on her own. She spent her later years in the United States as a patron of the visual arts and a crusader for the cause of world peace.

> "'Yes,' and never 'no' was our answer to the fabulous twenties. We built a gossamer bridge from war to war, as unreal as it was fragile, a passionate *passerelle* between a rejected past and an impossible future. Perhaps no such span of years (only two whizzing decades) have ever so amazed and disturbed a generation. Harry Crosby and I briefed the pattern of our times and, unknowingly, we drew the most surrealistic picture of them all."
>
> CARESSE CROSBY
> *The Passionate Years*, 1953

Iva Toguri d'Aquino (1916–)
Accused traitor

DURING WORLD WAR II, AN ENGLISH-LANGUAGE radio program called "Zero Hour" was broadcast by the Japanese to American troops in the Pacific. In addition to music and entertainment, the show included messages intended to destroy the Americans' morale and encourage them to surrender. The hosts of the program, all women, came to be known collectively as "Tokyo Rose."

One of the women was Iva Toguri d'Aquino, an American citizen of Japanese descent. After graduating from the University of California at Los Angeles in 1941, she had gone to visit a sick relative in Japan. The bombing of Pearl Harbor later that year brought the United States into the war. Considered an enemy alien, d'Aquino was forbidden to go home. She found work at Radio Tokyo and began broadcasting for "Zero Hour" in November 1943. After the war, journalists identified her as "Tokyo Rose," and she was put on trial for treason in the United States.

In 1949 d'Aquino was found guilty and served six years in prison. Later, new information came to light. D'Aquino claimed that, along with other prisoners of war, she had attempted to sabotage the broadcasts with hidden messages showing support for the Allies. She had refused to become a Japanese citizen and had been harassed for her pro-American views. In 1977 President Gerald Ford granted her a pardon.

Virginia Dare (1587–?)
First American-born colonist

IN MAY 1587 ELEANOR AND ANANIAS DARE LEFT England with over 100 others on an expedition sponsored by Sir Walter Raleigh. They had intended to establish a settlement in the Chesapeake Bay area but landed instead on Roanoke Island, then part of Virginia (now off the coast of North Carolina). Their little girl—the first child born in the New World to European parents—arrived on August 18 and was named after the colony. Nine days later Virginia's grandfather and the governor of the colony, John White, returned to England to obtain assistance and supplies for the struggling settlement.

Delayed by a war between England and Spain, White returned three years later to find that the settlers had disappeared, leaving only the word *croatoan* carved on a post. He and the ship's crew searched as much as they could, braving rough seas. However, no trace of the "Lost Colony" was found, even on the nearby island of Croatan, formerly the home of friendly Indians but by then deserted. For years afterward stories were told of white people living among the Native Americans, but none were ever seen. Virginia's tale, one of hope, disappointment, and mystery, has become the subject of art and literature.

Grace Darling (1815–1842)
Folk heroine

GRACE DARLING EXPECTED TO LEAD A QUIET, domestic life. She was the seventh of nine children, all of whom were brought up to be strictly religious by their stern, overbearing father. Grace was chosen to serve as the unofficial assistant to her father, the lighthouse keeper on Longstone, one of the Farne Islands off the rugged coast of Northumberland, England. The events of September 7, 1838, changed her life dramatically.

On that night the steamboat *Forfarshire* was wrecked in a storm. Showing skill, courage, and considerable physical strength, Grace rowed with her father in a small boat through dangerous seas to rescue five survivors. Suddenly she was a celebrity, sought after by journalists, poets, portrait painters,

Grace Darling and her father row out to the sinking boat.

and tourists. She was showered with gifts, requests for locks of her hair, proposals of marriage, and even an invitation to join a circus. The shy woman shunned the attention and continued to live on her island until her death from tuberculosis at an early age.

Emily Wilding Davison (1872–1913)
Militant suffragist

EMILY DAVISON WAS A MILITANT ENGLISH suffragist who believed strongly in the motto of Emmeline Pankhurst's group, the Women's Social and Political Union: "Deeds, not words." Having joined the union in 1906, she showed how she felt about not being able to vote by throwing stones, setting mailboxes on fire, and heckling politicians. She was imprisoned eight times and was brutally force-fed by jailers 49 times when she continued her protests by staging hunger strikes. While being held in Strangeways prison, she barricaded herself in her cell. In order to frighten her, prison officials began filling the cell with water, but Davison refused to unblock the door. It had to be broken down before she drowned. She later won a legal case against the prison for its harsh treatment.

Convinced that her cause needed a martyr, Emily attempted suicide by throwing herself down an iron staircase. Although she suffered serious injuries, she survived. She achieved tragic success in 1913, when she ran onto the track during the Derby Day race at Epsom Downs and was trampled by a horse owned by King George V. Most of the public considered her a crazy fanatic, but her funeral procession turned into one of the largest demonstration marches of the women's suffrage movement. Five years later British women over age 30 gained the right to vote, and in 1928 the age limit was lowered to 21.

Phoolan Devi (1955?–)
Bandit, folk hero, politician

PHOOLAN DEVI BECAME INDIA'S MOST NOTORIOUS modern-day *dacoit* (bandit) queen, responsible for more than 50 murders, for ambushing travelers, and for raiding villages in the Chambal River Valley of Uttar Pradesh. Devi turned to violence as a way to

avenge the pain she'd suffered as a girl. At age 11 she had been sold into marriage by her low-caste Hindu family in exchange for a cow and a bicycle. She repeatedly ran away from her abusive husband but was shunned by her family and assaulted by the local police. In 1979 she was kidnapped by a dacoit gang. Phoolan felt at home with the bandits, learned their skills, and eventually came to lead her own gang. Once rival dacoits of a higher caste captured and abused her, but she escaped and took revenge by murdering 20 high-caste men.

In India, especially in rural areas, tradition continues to condemn many Hindus born into low castes to lives of poverty and abuse. Phoolan became a heroine in the eyes of the oppressed. Her tale was told in song, in print, and on the screen. In 1983 she turned herself over to the authorities in a dramatic ceremony attended by thousands of fans. After 11 years in prison, she emerged to champion the people again, this time as a politician. She was elected to the Indian Parliament in 1996.

Jenny Diver (1700–1740)
Pickpocket

JENNY DIVER POSSESSED DEXTEROUS FINGERS, beauty, a gift for concocting clever schemes, and a total lack of morals. By picking pockets on the streets, she collected enough money to masquerade

A Pickpocket's Tricks

Jenny Diver's brazen schemes demonstrate what a fearless scam artist she was. One of her tactics was to disguise herself as a pregnant noblewoman and mingle with holiday crowds. Then suddenly she would pretend to faint. As spectators rushed to her aid, she and her "servant" accomplice helped themselves to the samaritans' jewels and purses. Another favorite trick was to go to church wearing a special dress with false arms attached. The costume left her real hands free to snatch whatever she could while those seated near her prayed.

as a rich lady. In this disguise she gained entrance to mansions, theaters, and other places where rich people gathered so she could rob them.

Born Mary Jones in Ireland, she had been raised in foster homes and had earned a good living as a seamstress, again thanks to her nimble fingers. Moving to London in hopes of becoming rich, she joined a gang of thieves who were so impressed by her skill that they gave her the name Jenny Diver—*diver* was the popular slang for "pickpocket." These mentors eventually became her assistants and secured her release from prison by bribing officials whenever she was arrested. In 1738 Diver was unable to escape conviction and was banished to Virginia. Within a year she had returned, but she was no longer as nimble as she once had been. Her next arrest, in 1740, led to a death sentence. She was hanged at Tyburn before a large crowd, who refrained from their usual taunting and cheering, so in awe were they of the greatest pickpocket in history.

Jessica Dubroff (1988–1996)
Child pilot

ON APRIL 11, 1996, SEVEN-YEAR-OLD JESSICA Dubroff took off from the Cheyenne, Wyoming, airport at the controls of a single-engine Cessna airplane. It was the third day of her attempt to be the youngest pilot to fly across the continental United States. Her father, Lloyd Dubroff, who had suggested the feat, was in the plane, along with flight instructor Joe Reid. Jessica was optimistic, although veteran flyers had misgivings about the icy, stormy weather. Shortly after takeoff, the overloaded plane's engine stalled, and it crashed onto a residential street, killing all three onboard.

The media had been following Jessica's story closely. Growing up in Pescadero, California, she and her brother and sister were homeschooled and didn't even own a television. Jessica learned carpentry, rode horses, and played several musical instruments. After the accident, though, the glowing headlines turned to criticism. Jessica's parents were faulted for encouraging her to attempt the stunt after only four months of lessons. Many people thought media pressure had influenced the decision to continue in bad weather. Still others—a minority—defended Jessica's mother, who maintained that she and her husband had wanted their daughter to pursue her dreams, not limit them because of fear.

Lady Agnes Randolph Dunbar (1313?–1369?)
Folk heroine

FOR CENTURIES SCOTLAND BATTLED TO MAINTAIN independence, while England fought to bring its northern neighbor back under control. In 1338 the fortress of Patrick Dunbar, Earl of Dunbar and March, was one of the few castles left in Scottish hands. The earl rode off to fight the English in the field, leaving the castle's defense to his wife, Agnes.

Agnes was a relative of the famed Scottish leader Robert the Bruce, and she was the daughter of Thomas Randolph, Earl of Moray, a longtime foe of the English. She was more than capable of directing the defense of her home. When troops led by the British Earl of Salisbury laid siege to Dunbar Castle, she endured hardships along with her people. She showed great bravado, laughing at the attackers and instructing her maids to dust the battlements after each assault. Five months later, the English gave up and went away. The heroism of "Black Agnes," as she came to be known, was celebrated in folk songs and prose, including the writing of Sir Walter Scott.

Simone ("Mama Doc") Duvalier (1913?–1997)
Political matriarch

SIMONE OVIDE WAS RAISED IN AN ORPHANAGE outside Port-au-Prince, Haiti, and was working as a nurse's aide when she met Dr. François Duvalier. After their marriage she helped François rise in politics until he became "President for Life" in 1957. She then took an active role in "Papa Doc" Duvalier's dictatorship, which was known for its corruption and brutality. Many Haitians suffered and died so that the Duvaliers and their supporters could live in luxury. Vain, haughty Simone cultivated the image of a benefactress, but the people only feared her.

After Papa Doc died in 1971, his teenaged son, Jean-Claude ("Baby Doc"), took his place. Simone, who already wielded considerable power, now ruled Haiti in all but name through her easily dominated son. In 1981 Simone's reign came to an end when Baby Doc married Michele Bennett, who was as ruthless as her mother-in-law. Five years later, a political coup forced Jean-Claude to flee to France with his mother and wife. Michele abandoned her impoverished husband soon afterward. Simone died in poverty, longing to return to the power she had known in Haiti.

Simone Duvalier with "Papa Doc" Duvalier

Sarah Emma Edmonds (1841–1898)
Union soldier

ONE OF THE MANY WOMEN WHO DISGUISED themselves as men in order to fight in the Civil War, Sarah Edmonds won the admiration of her fellow soldiers, who had no idea that she wasn't really "Franklin Thompson." Born in New Brunswick, Canada, she later settled in Flint, Michigan, where she adopted a male identity and worked as a Bible salesman. After joining the 2nd Michigan Infantry, Edmonds participated in the Battle of Blackburn's Ford and the First Battle of Bull Run and served as an aide to Colonel Orlando Poe. She went on intelligence missions "disguised" as a woman and as an African slave, although the latter disguise was nearly ruined when the heat caused her to sweat and the skin dye to run.

Perhaps because she caught malaria and feared discovery if she went to the infirmary, Edmonds deserted in early 1863 and went to work as a nurse. In 1865 she published *Nurse and Spy in the Union Army*, a sensational account of her experiences. When she applied for a veteran's pension in 1882, her former comrades supported her petition. She was the only woman ever to be made a member of the Grand Army of the Republic (a society of Union army veterans).

Ruth Ellis (1926–1955)
Murderer

RUTH ELLIS HAD VERY POOR TASTE IN MEN. BY THE age of 27, the platinum blonde had borne a child out of wedlock and divorced an abusive, alcoholic husband. She was working as a night club manager in London when she met David Blakely, a racecar driver, and the two began a passionate affair. Blakely was like the other men in her life; he, too, drank hard and beat her. Still, Ellis found it impossible to leave him.

On the evening of April 10, 1955, Ellis took a cab to the Hampstead pub where Blakely had been drinking and fatally shot him. At her trial she frankly admitted that she had been furious with Blakely and intended to kill him; she also stated that she had loved him and wanted to die as punishment for her crime. The jury deliberated for less than half an hour before returning a guilty verdict, and she was sen-

bishop and returned to the nun's habit. She also returned to Spain, where she was considered a heroine for her adventures, received a pension from King Philip IV, and had an audience with Pope Urban VIII. The lure of New Spain was strong, though, and eventually de Erauso left the convent again. She lived her last years as a mule-train driver in Mexico, brawling until the end.

Esther (5th century B.C.E.?)
Biblical heroine

THE STORY OF ESTHER IS TOLD IN THE OLD Testament book named for its heroine. Although historians have found no other evidence of Esther's existence, a major character in the tale is the Persian King Ahasuerus, believed to be Xerxes I. Ahasuerus was conducting a search for a new queen. One of the candidates was Esther, a young woman raised in the city of Susa by her cousin Mordecai. After one look at Esther's beauty, the king chose her for his bride. On Mordecai's advice she kept her Jewish origins a secret. Later Mordecai angered the grand vizier, Haman, who plotted to destroy not only Mordecai, but all the Jews in Persia. The king signed an edict ordering the slaughter.

Esther invited Haman and the king to a banquet, where she dramatically announced that she was

tenced to hang. Although capital punishment opponents fought to save her, she was executed on July 13. Ellis was the last woman hanged in Great Britain. The government abolished that method of execution the following year.

Catalina de Erauso (1592?–1652?)
Soldier, adventurer

YOUNG CATALINA DE ERAUSO WAS SENT TO LIVE IN a convent by her noble Spanish family, but the life of a nun held no interest for her. Instead she ran away, disguised herself as a boy, and joined an expedition to the New World. Hot-tempered, fearless, and strong, Catalina apparently had no trouble maintaining her male identity. She wandered through Peru, Chile, and Mexico, becoming famous for her sword-fighting, a necessary skill on the frontier. She spent many years as a soldier battling Indians and achieved the rank of captain. She also developed a habit of getting into fights over card games or romantic interests, then having to run from the law.

In 1622, facing execution for one of her escapades, de Erauso revealed her identity to a

Esther bows before King Ahasuerus.

Jewish and that the plot to massacre the Jews was a cruel act of revenge by Haman. The king, by then devoted to Esther, ordered Haman to be hanged on the gallows originally built for Mordecai's execution. The edict commanding the massacre could not be revoked, so the king allowed the Jews to arm and defend themselves. Jews still celebrate Esther's bravery and this ancient victory over the Persians at the festival of Purim.

Marian Anthon Fish (1853–1915)
Socialite

"MAMIE" ANTHON WAS THE DAUGHTER OF A distinguished New York City lawyer who left his family nearly destitute at his death. Her 1876 marriage to Stuyvesant Fish, the future president of the Illinois Central Railroad, brought her wealth. She used her money, along with her talent for organization, to become one of society's most popular hostesses. She began giving dinner parties at her Manhattan townhouse, her country estate on the Hudson River, and her mansion-sized "cottage" in fashionable Newport, Rhode Island. Her affectionate husband supported her endeavors but often retreated to quieter surroundings during his wife's lively gatherings.

Impatient and quick-tempered, Mrs. Stuyvesant Fish (as she was known in society) was renowned for her tart tongue and her irreverent attitude toward

Wild Parties

Bored by the strict, upper-class social customs of her day, Mamie Fish made her own rules. Instead of the three-hour dinners hosted by most society matrons, Fish introduced the 50-minute meal. Footmen raced around the dinner table, clearing and replenishing plates at record speed. Guests who dawdled or became involved in conversations risked having their plates whisked away. Fish also enjoyed coming up with absurd themes for her gatherings. At one lavish party, she insisted that everyone speak in baby talk.

the stodgy customs of the social elite. She loved playing practical jokes and once invited a group of distinguished guests to meet a prince, who turned out to be a monkey dressed in evening clothes. Determined to be the most excessive at excess, she once hired the entire Barnum & Bailey Circus sideshow to perform at a party. Many popular entertainers performed after her dinners, including dancers Irene and Vernon Castle, who were paid a small fortune to invent a new dance—the Fish Glide—in their hostess' honor.

Margaret Fox (1833?–1893)

Kate Fox (1839?–1892)
Spiritualists

MARGARET AND KATE FOX WERE YOUNG GIRLS when their family moved into a supposedly haunted farmhouse near Rochester, New York, in 1847. Soon after, strange knockings and tappings began to be heard. The sisters claimed that the sounds were made by spirits and that they could communicate with them by an eerie code, later known as "Rochester rapping." Curious observers flocked to the Fox house, and the spiritualist movement was born. Margaret and Kate, with the help of their older sister, Leah, would be America's foremost mediums for four decades, making small fortunes off the gullible converts who attended their séances and inspiring dozens of other spiritualists.

The Fox sisters established themselves in New York City and toured America and England, adding ghostly materializations and spirit writing to their repertoire. They won over famous politicians and intellectuals, as well as ordinary people who were anxious to communicate with the dead. The newspaper editor Horace Greeley endorsed them. Margaret entered into a highly publicized romance with arctic explorer Elisha Kane and, after his death in 1857, used the name Mrs. Kane. Kate married a British barrister, H. D. Jencken, in 1872. By then the sisters were suffering from the burden of celebrity and had become alcoholics.

In 1888 Margaret publicly confessed that their claims were all a hoax, begun as a joke on their superstitious mother. They had made the rapping sounds with their toes. Spiritualist true believers refused to accept the confession, though, and neither sister completely abandoned her career as a medium. Both Kate and Margaret died impoverished in New York.

Mary Frith (Moll Cutpurse) (1584?–1659)
Thief, fence

MARY FRITH STARTED OUT AS A PICKPOCKET (OR "cutpurse") in London and earned her famous nickname at an early age. After being caught several times, Moll disguised herself in men's clothes and took to the roads as a highway robber. A term in Newgate prison convinced her to turn to a safer profession. She opened a shop on Fleet Street, where she bought and sold stolen goods. Rightful owners sometimes came to buy back their own property after reading Moll's advertisements.

Moll Cutpurse was a notorious figure in the early 17th century underworld and a popular character with the public, who appreciated her high spirits and impudence. She was arrested for singing rude songs and wearing men's clothes but went right on drinking, cursing, smoking, and wielding a sword like a man. During her lifetime she was featured in the 1611 play *The Roaring Girl*, by Thomas Dekker and Thomas Middleton. Other literary tributes followed. Moll published an autobiography of her own, too, though most of it was the product of her imagination. Despite her rough life, she lived into her 70s.

Lynnette Alice ("Squeaky") Fromme (1952–)
Would-be assassin

SQUEAKY FROMME WAS A MEMBER OF CHARLES Manson's "family," a cultlike group who believed Manson could solve the world's problems with free love, drugs, and death. Manson and several of his followers were convicted of murdering seven people, including movie actress Sharon Tate, in 1969. While he served a life sentence in prison, Fromme remained his most devoted supporter and spokeswoman outside. She was arrested several times but only convicted once—for trying to block testimony at the murder trial by putting the hallucinogenic drug LSD in a witness' hamburger.

On September 5, 1975, President Gerald Ford was shaking hands with the public at a rally in front of the California State Capitol in Sacramento. Fromme managed to get within two feet of the president and point a gun at him, but when she pulled the trigger, it didn't go off. She was quickly subdued by bodyguards, who surrounded the shaken president. Fromme, who had committed the crime in an attempt to draw attention to Manson, was the first person convicted of attempted assassination of a president and was imprisoned for life. She escaped from her West Virginia prison in 1987 but was recaptured less than two days later.

Myra Clark Gaines (1805–1885)
Litigant

MYRA CLARK GAINES WAS THE ILLEGITIMATE daughter of Daniel Clark, a wealthy New Orleans businessman. She was raised by a trusted friend of her father's in Delaware and didn't learn of

her parentage until after Clark died, leaving his fortune to his mother. Myra, then married to William Whitney and a mother of three, decided she'd been deprived of her inheritance. In 1835 she brought her first legal suit to reclaim it. The case would drag on for 56 years.

During the course of the record-setting legal battle, Myra employed 30 lawyers, many of whom worked with her for their entire careers. After her first husband died, she married General Edmund Gaines in 1839, promising him $100,000 if he helped her win the case. The Supreme Court at first upheld her claim, then reversed its decision in 1851, but she continued to fight. She angered her home city of New Orleans, which by then owned many of the properties in question. Myra even stooped to forging a "lost will" and trying to prove that her parents had secretly married. Reduced to poverty, she struggled on but didn't live to hear the final verdict. Six years after her death, her heirs were awarded more than $500,000 from Daniel Clark's estate.

Gallus Mag (19th century)
Thug

During the mid-19th century, the Fourth Ward of New York City was filled with tenements and taverns, the home of vicious gangs, river pirates, and disease-carrying rats. One of its most notorious taverns was the Hole-in-the-Wall on Water Street, operated by gangster One-Armed Charley Monell and his two henchwomen, Kate Flannery and Gallus Mag.

Born in England, Gallus Mag got her nickname because she used suspenders (or "galluses") to hold up her skirt. Her real name is no longer known. If a tavern customer got out of hand, Mag grabbed his ear between her teeth and dragged him to the door. If he really misbehaved, she bit off his ear and added it to the others she kept preserved in a jar of alcohol behind the bar. In addition to her bouncing duties, Mag was a mugger on the waterfront, wielding her pistol and bludgeon with surprising savagery. She disappeared after the authorities finally closed the Hole-in-the-Wall, but she has remained a legend of old New York.

Dorothy "Dolly" Gee (1897–1978)
Embezzler

Dolly Gee, born Chang Hor-gee, emigrated with her family from China to San Francisco in 1901. Despite racial prejudice, Gee's father was placed in charge of Chinese people's accounts at the Bank of America. In 1914 Gee began helping her father with the accounts, which were written in Chinese, and she went around Chinatown encouraging people to place their money in the bank. Father and daughter were so successful that the Bank of America opened a branch in Chinatown and put them in charge. The family became rich and prominent, thanks to Gee's devotion to her career. She ran the bank after her father's retirement in 1929 and was honored as the first woman banker in America.

In 1963, the year she planned to retire, Gee shocked her community by confessing that she and her father had embezzled nearly $400,000 over the course of 50 years. They had juggled the accounts in order to pay off debts incurred by their speculative investments in foreign banks and gambling losses. Gee was sentenced to five years in prison and released after 16 months; she then disappeared from public view.

Mildred Gillars ("Axis Sally") (1900–1988)
Propagandist, traitor

American troops stationed in Europe during World War II listened on short-wave radio to English-language music and talk shows, enjoying nostalgic songs such as "Lili Marlene." These shows were interspersed with Nazi propaganda messages intended to destroy morale, including anti-Semitic tirades and hints that wives and sweethearts back home were being unfaithful. A chilling drama detailing the horrors awaiting the Allies was broadcast just before the Normandy invasion. The woman responsible for this and other Radio Berlin programs was American citizen Mildred Gillars, whose nickname was "Axis Sally."

Gillars, an aspiring actress, had moved to Germany in 1934 to study music and found work teaching English. Her sultry voice proved ideal for broadcasting. She was soon hired by Radio Berlin and began to produce her propandistic programs.

Brought to trial after the war, Gillars was convicted of treason, although she claimed she was driven to make the broadcasts by her love for Max Otto Koischwitz, a member of the German Foreign Ministry staff. She was released from prison in 1961 and thereafter taught at a convent school in Columbus, Ohio.

Lady Godiva (?–1080?)
Heroine

THE FAMOUS STORY OF LADY GODIVA IS MORE legend than truth. It has been retold many times in art and literature, most notably in a poem by Alfred, Lord Tennyson. However, there might well be some historical basis for it. There was a Lady Godiva—or Godgifu. She was an Anglo-Saxon noblewoman, the wife of Leofric, Earl of Mercia.

Leofric was an important leader during the reigns of the early English kings Canute and Edward the Confessor. He and his wife were generous supporters of the Christian church, founding a monastery in their home city of Coventry in 1043 and endowing several others. But Leofric imposed heavy taxes on the people of Coventry. Legend holds that Godiva, sympathetic to the people's plight, begged her husband to ease their burden. He responded that he would do so if she would ride naked through the city streets, never suspecting that she would rise to the challenge. With her long hair strategically arranged, Godiva rode through town on horseback, having asked the people to remain indoors and avert their gazes. The citizens were happy to allow their heroine her modesty, all except a tailor who was nicknamed Peeping Tom and struck blind for daring to peek.

Rose O'Neal Greenhow (1817–1864)
Confederate spy

ROSE O'NEAL GREENHOW, A BEAUTIFUL WIDOW, was a hostess moving in the highest social circles of Washington, D.C., when the Civil War began in 1861. A native of Maryland, Greenhow was a supporter of slavery, as were many members of the upper class in that state. She remained in the North to help the Confederates by passing on secret military information, which she gathered from the Union government officials who were her friends and admirers. In August 1861 she was arrested by Allan Pinkerton, head of the Union intelligence service, who

"The Capitol . . . had been made one of the strongest fortified cities of the world. . . . The most skillful detectives were summoned from far and near, to trace the steps of maids and matrons. For several weeks I had been followed, and my house watched, by those emissaries of the State Department, the detective police. This was often a subject of amusement to me; and several times, when accompanied by my young friend Miss Mackall, we would turn and follow those who we fancied were giving us an undue share of attention."

ROSE O'NEAL GREENHOW
My Imprisonment and the First Year of Abolition Rule at Washington, 1863

had grown suspicious of her activities. Greenhow managed to continue sending information from prison, but she was expelled from the North in 1862.

The South welcomed her as a heroine, and the Confederate president, Jefferson Davis, sent her on a diplomatic mission to Europe, where she published her memoirs. In 1864 she attempted to return to the Confederacy, but her ship went aground while running the Union blockade off North Carolina. Fleeing in a lifeboat, Greenhow, who was carrying a heavy bag of gold coins, was drowned when the boat overturned in the rough seas. She was given a military funeral.

Lady Jane Grey (1537–1554)
The "nine days' queen" of England

DURING THE 16TH CENTURY IN EUROPE, THE supremacy of Roman Catholicism was challenged by the rise of Protestantism in a movement that is now called the Reformation. In England this tumultuous transition was initiated by King Henry VIII, whose efforts to beget a son led him to marry six times—and to break away from Roman Catholicism because divorce was forbidden. The pope had long been considered the spiritual leader of the Church of

England, but Henry declared that he would rule the church as well as the country. After Henry's death, his sister's granddaughter, Lady Jane Grey, became a pawn in the dangerous game of political intrigue played by followers of the rival religions.

Lady Jane's father, the Duke of Suffolk, was anxious to keep the throne in Protestant hands. King Edward VI was sickly, and his sister and heir, Mary, was a staunch Catholic. A plan to marry Edward to the devoutly Protestant Jane failed, but the young king was persuaded to defy tradition and declare her his successor.

Jane, however, had no interest in ruling. She was a scholar, who preferred studying languages and having theological discussions. Upon hearing of Edward's death in 1553, she fainted. On July 19, nine days after Jane was named queen, Mary claimed the throne. Jane gladly gave it to her. She was condemned to death for treason, although it seemed certain she would be pardoned. Then her father took part in a rebellion led by one of his allies, Thomas Wyatt. Enraged, Mary decided to rid herself of the troublesome family. She ordered Jane and her young husband, Guildford Dudley, beheaded. The Duke of Suffolk was executed the following week. There was great public sympathy for the 17-year-old girl, who had been forced into treason against her will.

Frances Griffiths (1907?–1986)

Elsie Wright (1902–1988)
Hoaxers

IN JULY 1917 FRANCES GRIFFITHS AND HER COUSIN, Elsie Wright, went on a walk in Cottingley Glen near their home in Yorkshire, England, with a borrowed camera. They came back with a glass plate negative which, when developed, showed Frances surrounded by four dancing fairies. Another photograph, taken in September, depicted Elsie with a gnome. Two years later Elsie's mother mentioned the photographs to the Theosophist lecturer Edward Gardner, who in turn showed them to Sir Arthur Conan Doyle, author of the Sherlock Holmes mysteries and an advocate of spiritualism. Doyle published an article in *Strand* magazine in 1920 announcing that fairies had been photographed. It caused a sensation among believers and doubters alike.

Frances Griffiths and the fairies

Gardner encouraged the girls to make three more photographs and had all five examined by "experts," who pronounced them authentic. The story went unchallenged until an expert at the Kodak company reexamined the photos in 1978 using modern methods and found several inconsistencies. Frances and Elsie, by then elderly women, stuck to their story until 1981, when Frances finally confessed that they had cut pictures out of a children's book and used hatpins to hold them in place. However, both maintained that they had seen real fairies and that the fifth photograph, which depicts fairies but not the girls, was genuine. "The Cottingley Fairies Hoax" was a practical joke that got out of hand when the girls realized that their confession would disappoint the many people who believed in fairies.

Belle Gunness (1860–1908?)
Serial killer

IN 1901 BELLE GUNNESS, THE DAUGHTER OF Norwegian immigrants, moved to a hog farm near La Porte, Indiana. To her neighbors she seemed to be a respectable, hardworking widow, her husband having died in an "accident." Gunness began advertising in Chicago newspapers for a new husband who was wealthy and willing to help pay off her mortgage. Fourteen men applied for the position—and were never seen alive again.

When the Gunness farmhouse burned down in 1908, four bodies were found inside. Three of them belonged to Belle's children. The authorities became suspicious when they noticed that the fourth body, which had been identified as Belle's, was smaller than her 280 pounds—and missing a head. They began to sift through the charred remains of the farmhouse and found what was left of her would-be suitors. It was estimated that she had stolen a small fortune from the men after murdering them. Belle's farm helper, Ray Lamphere, was convicted of burning the farmhouse, which became a grisly tourist attraction. He later confessed that he had helped dispose of the bodies. He died in prison in 1911, but Gunness was never found.

Nell Gwyn (1650–1687)
Actress, royal mistress

NELL GWYN WAS RARE AMONG ROYAL MISTRESSES: The people of England loved her. She represented a new era, now known as the Restoration, which began when King Charles II ascended the throne. Charles's coronation ended a period during which England's government had been controlled by Puritans under the leadership of Oliver Cromwell. The Restoration period was lively and devoted to

pleasure, much like Gwyn herself. The people appreciated her lack of pretension—she kept her childhood friends even after she became famous—as well as the role she played in encouraging the king to establish Chelsea Hospital.

Growing up in poor and disreputable circumstances, Nell had made her living selling oranges outside the Theatre Royal in London's Drury Lane until she became an actress at age 15. She soon found success on the stage, particularly in comedies. Although almost completely illiterate, she was witty and high-spirited enough to become a society favorite. She became one of the king's mistresses in 1669. Because she could keep him entertained and relaxed, she kept her place in his affections, despite heavy competition, until his death in 1685. Gwyn's two sons by the king became the Duke of St. Albans and Lord Beauclerc.

Virginia Hall (1906–1982)
Allied spy

VIRGINIA HALL, A FORMER DEBUTANTE FROM Baltimore, was working as a clerk at the American embassy in Warsaw, Poland, when she lost most of her left leg in a hunting accident in 1931. It seemed that her dream of becoming a foreign service diplomat was shattered, but, undaunted, she went on to become one of the most successful Allied spies of World War II. Known as "The Limping Lady," she would be anxiously hunted by the Nazis.

In June 1940 Hall joined the British Special Operations Executive and was trained in radio operation, sabotage, and guerrilla warfare. When Germany invaded France, she was working with the French underground resistance. She was forced to flee across the Pyrenees in the bitter cold on foot—a difficult task with a wooden leg. Hall then joined America's Office of Strategic Services and returned to France. During the day she masqueraded as a peasant milkmaid, disguising her limp. At night she passed on important information by radio and Morse code. After the war she became the first civilian woman to receive the Distinguished Service Cross, America's second highest military honor. In 1950 Hall married a French-born fellow agent, Paul Goillot. She went on to work for the Central Intelligence Agency until her mandatory retirement at age 60.

Lady Emma Hamilton (1761?–1815)
Adventuress

BY THE TIME SHE WAS 20 YEARS OLD, AMY LYON, the daughter of an English village blacksmith, had adopted a new name, Emma Hart, and a new station in life as the mistress of various wealthy men. She was living happily with Charles Greville in 1786 when his uncle, Sir William Hamilton, fell for her charms. Hamilton, the British envoy to the Kingdom of Naples, agreed to pay off Greville's debts if Emma would come live with him. She reluctantly agreed. Four years later she was Hamilton's wife and the toast of Neapolitan society. The renowned beauty posed for famous artists and played an important role in her powerful husband's political and diplomatic affairs, becoming a close friend of Queen Maria Carolina of Naples.

In 1793 Emma met Admiral Horatio Nelson, a British naval officer who would become a hero fighting Napoléon Bonaparte. She used her diplomatic skills to help Nelson win an important battle, and they soon became lovers. When the Hamiltons returned to England in 1800, Nelson followed Emma, who was secretly pregnant with his daughter. After William Hamilton's death, she lived with Nelson until he died at the Battle of Trafalgar in

1805. Both men left her money, but it wasn't enough to support her lavish lifestyle. After spending time in a debtor's prison, Emma left England. She died an exile in France.

Florence Kling Harding (1860–1924)
First lady

FLORENCE KLING GREW UP STRONG-WILLED AND independent, constantly at odds with her demanding father, the richest man in small-town Marion, Ohio. He disapproved of her first marriage and wouldn't allow her to return home when it ended in divorce in 1886. Florence supported herself and her son by giving music lessons. She eventually reconciled with her father, but, at the age of 30, she again infuriated him by marrying Warren G. Harding, editor of the struggling *Star* newspaper. Florence took over the *Star*'s circulation department and, thanks to her energy and discipline, made it a success. Warren used his growing popularity as a springboard into politics, a move wholeheartedly supported by his wife. Campaigning tirelessly, she was partly responsible for his election to the United States Senate in 1915 and to the presidency in 1920.

Once in the White House, however, Florence's efforts couldn't overcome the damage done to Warren's reputation by the rampant corruption in his administration. Her own ambition and energy caused many people to dislike her. In addition, although he often deferred to her, calling her his "Duchess,"

Warren engaged in several not-very-secret extramarital affairs. When he died suddenly during a visit to California, rumors flew that the first lady was in some way responsible—even though doctors confirmed that he had suffered a heart attack. Florence died the following year.

Jean Struven Harris (1923–)
Homicide

JEAN HARRIS MET DR. HERMAN TARNOWER IN 1966. Harris, a divorced mother of two, was the headmistress of the selective Madeira School for girls in McLean, Virginia. Tarnower was a successful cardiologist. The two began an affair. Although Tarnower promised marriage, he continued to see other women. He wanted Jean's help in editing the book that would make him famous—the hugely popular and profitable *Complete Scarsdale Medical Diet* (1979). However, as soon as it was published and became a best-seller, he told her the affair was over. Devastated, Harris shot Tarnower to death on March 10, 1980. She claimed at her sensational trial that she had intended to kill herself and that Tarnower had been shot by mistake in a struggle for the gun. Still, she was convicted of murder and sentenced to 15 years' imprisonment.

Harris was paroled after 13 years, due to good behavior and the threat of a serious heart condition. While in prison, she authored *They Always Call Us Ladies* (1988), and since her release she has lectured on prison reform and raised funds for the education of prisoners' children. She now lives a quiet life in New Hampshire.

Nancy Hart (1735?–1830)
Revolutionary heroine

AROUND 1771 NANCY HART AND HER HUSBAND and children moved to Georgia, the site of some of the fiercest fighting in the American Revolution. The colonists supporting independence were known as Whigs; those who were loyal to England were the Tories. Poor, illiterate, and a staunch Whig, Nancy undertook deeds of such bravery that she became a heroine, praised in art and legend. A county in Georgia is even named after her.

In the most famous tale of Hart's valor, about five Tories shot her last turkey and demanded that she roast it for them. While her young daughter ran off to alert the neighbors, Nancy poured generous servings of whiskey for the men and secretly tossed three of their rifles outside before grabbing a gun to defend herself. She killed one man, wounded another, and held the remaining Tories captive until patriot friends arrived to take them to the woods and hang them. Nancy became known for other adventures, too. She is said to have crossed a rushing river on a log raft to bring back information from the enemy camp. After the war was over, Hart moved to Kentucky and lived to be well into her 90s.

Pearl Hart (1871?–1925?)
Stagecoach robber

AS A YOUNG WOMAN, PEARL HART FELL IN LOVE with the myth of the Wild West and left her husband, Frederick, to seek adventure in Colorado and Arizona. Twice she visited her family in Ontario, Canada. She and Frederick also attempted to reconcile and had two children together. But, in the end, she returned to the outlaw life.

Hart was living in Globe, Arizona, working as a small-time mugger with a miner named Joe Boot, when she received word that her mother needed money for medical bills. To raise the funds, the partners held up a stagecoach on May 30, 1899, taking about $450 from the passengers. Unfortunately they had forgotten to plan their getaway. They got lost in the hills and were easily captured. Pearl was sentenced to five years at the all-male prison at Yuma. As the only woman to rob a stagecoach and, it would turn out, the last known person to do so in the United States, she became a celebrity—a role she enjoyed. She was released after 18 months' imprisonment, and nothing certain is known about her later life.

Patricia Hearst (1954–)
Kidnapping victim, robber

ON FEBRUARY 5, 1974, 19-YEAR-OLD PATRICIA (Patty) Hearst, the granddaughter of media tycoon William Randolph Hearst, was kidnapped. The men who broke down the door of her Berkeley, California, apartment and shoved her into the trunk of a car belonged to the Symbionese Liberation Army (SLA), a small group of radical terrorists led by escaped convict Donald DeFreeze. They announced that Patty would be released if the wealthy Hearsts would, in addition to paying a ransom, provide millions of dollars' worth of free food to the poor. The Hearsts began distributing food, but not fast enough for the SLA.

Two months later Patty helped her captors rob a bank in San Francisco, and a shocked nation watched a television broadcast of security camera footage that showed her brandishing a machine gun. A taped message was released in which Hearst stated that she had joined the SLA and taken the name Tania. Many people thought she had been brainwashed; others suspected that she had been in league with the SLA even before her abduction. After 20 months on the run, Hearst was captured, tried, and sentenced to seven years in prison for bank robbery. Released after serving nearly two years, she married her former bodyguard, Bernard Shaw. In 1982 she published an autobiography, *Every Secret Thing*, in which she told her side of the story and described being brainwashed by her kidnappers. The Shaws now live in Connecticut with their two daughters.

> "... [I] would without hesitation precede or follow thee to the Vulcanian fires according to thy word. For not with me was my heart, but with thee. But now, more than ever, if it be not with thee, it is nowhere. For without thee it cannot anywhere exist."
>
> HÉLÖISE
> first letter to Abelard

Hélöise (1098?–1164)
Romantic heroine, writer, nun

HÉLÖISE WAS NOT AN ORDINARY UPPER-CLASS GIRL from medieval Paris: She was encouraged to read and study. Her family even hired the well-known philosopher Peter Abelard to be her tutor. However, when Hélöise and her teacher fell in love, secretly married, and had a son, her uncle was so enraged that he had his servants attack Abelard. Severely injured, Abelard entered a monastery in 1119, and Hélöise later became a nun, although she wrote to Abelard that she still loved him. His letters in response urged her to channel her emotions into religious faith, and they eventually began to correspond on theological matters.

After living in the convent of Argenteuil, Hélöise became the first abbess of the Paraclete, a religious community founded by Abelard. Under her skillful guidance, the abbey flourished. After her death Hélöise was buried beside Abelard. Their tragic romance has been the subject of literature and art. Their published letters, which contain their thoughts on love and religion, are considered great works in their own right.

Sally Hemings (1773–1835)
Slave

SALLY HEMINGS WAS BORN IN VIRGINIA, THE daughter of a white man named John Wayles and his slave, Elizabeth Hemings. Sally's father died the year of her birth, and she became the property of her half-sister, Martha, and Martha's husband, Thomas Jefferson, one of the principal authors of the Declaration of Independence and a future U.S. president. In 1787 Hemings accompanied Jefferson's daughter, Mary, on a trip to Paris. Two years later she returned to the Jefferson plantation, Monticello, and became the housekeeper there. Hemings had at least five children, four of whom survived. Her children were allowed more privileges than the other slaves and eventually gained their freedom. Hemings herself was probably granted an unofficial freedom, so that she could remain in Virginia after Jefferson's death in 1826 (the law required that freed slaves leave the state).

The facts of Hemings's life are overshadowed by speculations about the identity of her children's father. Was it Thomas Jefferson? If so, then one of the "fathers of the nation" kept his own children enslaved. This possibility has been debated in newspaper articles published at the time by Jefferson's political enemies and in folktales, books, and movies throughout the years. Results of DNA tests conducted in 1998 indicated that Jefferson was most likely the father of at least one of Hemings's children. It's difficult to know the truth about their relationship, obscured as it is by time and secrecy. However, the controversy has played an important role in discussions of the exploitation of female slaves.

Myra Hindley (1942–)
Murderer

IN 1961 MYRA HINDLEY SEEMED TO BE A NORMAL working-class girl. She was a typist for a chemical supply firm in Manchester, England, when she met and became infatuated with Ian Brady. He was a clerk in his mid-30s, who spent his lunch hours reading Adolf Hitler's *Mein Kampf* (My Struggle) and had a long history of petty crimes. The pair began a relationship based on their shared obsession with cruelty and obscenity. In 1963 they committed the first of what would become known as the "Moors Murders." They abducted, tortured, and murdered at least four young people between the ages of 10 and 17 and then buried them on Saddleworth Moor.

Hindley and Brady were arrested in October 1965 after they murdered a fifth victim in front of Hindley's brother-in-law, David Smith, who alerted the police. Their tendency to photograph and make audio recordings of their crimes led to their convictions in

1966 for three of the murders. Both were sentenced to life in prison. Hindley once tried to escape and has since attempted to obtain parole by claiming that she was only Brady's accomplice, but few support her cause. Most people believe she was an active participant in crimes that left a lasting memory of horror.

Hua Mu-Lan (5th century?)
Warrior

THE STORY OF CHINA'S GREATEST WOMAN WARRIOR is told in folktales, popular songs, and poetry. It is not known exactly when she lived or where, but many people believe that there is a historical basis to the legend of her exploits. Mu-Lan's father, who had no elder son, trained her in the fighting arts. When he was called to join the emperor's troops, he was so ill that Mu-Lan begged to be allowed to take his place. Her father refused, so she challenged him to a sword fight on the condition that, if she won, she could go to war using his name. She won the fight.

Disguised as a man, Mu-Lan not only hid her identity for 12 years but impressed her fellow warriors with her fierce bravery, skill in battle, and

leadership abilities. Her commanding officer viewed her so favorably that he offered his daughter in marriage. Mu-Lan turned down the proposal, as well as a chance at a prestigious government position, preferring to return to her home. There she resumed her life as a woman and fought no more.

Thérèse d'Aurignac Humbert (1860–1916)
Impostor

THÉRÈSE D'AURIGNAC, AN UNEDUCATED FRENCH washerwoman, was clever and ambitious. In 1877 she met—or claimed to have met—an American multimillionaire named Henry Crawford. According to her account, she nursed him back to health after an attack of food poisoning and, in return, he later willed his $20-million fortune to Thérèse and her younger sister. Thérèse also claimed that there were legal complications surrounding the will, so the inheritance had to be locked up in a safe in her bedroom until the case could be settled.

For the next 25 years, Thérèse led a luxurious life in Paris. Bankers loaned her huge sums, believing that she would be able to repay them—at high interest rates—once she was allowed to open the safe. She married a prominent lawyer, Frédéric Humbert, who was attracted to her wealth. After discovering her

deception, Frédéric became her accomplice, along with her sister and two brothers. The brothers kept the legal battle going by claiming to be Crawford's nephews and true heirs and bringing actual cases to court. In 1902 Thérèse's reluctance to see the matter settled finally aroused suspicions. She and her allies had fled by the time the safe was opened and discovered to contain little of value. The conspirators were captured in Spain, brought back to Paris, and found guilty of fraud.

"Poker" Alice Ivers (1851–1930)
Gambler

BORN IN ENGLAND AND RAISED IN VIRGINIA TO be a ladylike schoolteacher, "Poker" Alice moved to Leadville, Colorado, with her parents, who hoped to cash in on the gold rush. She earned her nickname in the high-class gambling parlors that she frequented with her mining engineer husband. After his death she turned to what she knew best and set out on the gambling circuit, drawing crowds and winning money with her skills as a cardsharper.

Ivers took to smoking cigars and settling arguments with a Colt revolver, declaring that she loved playing cards more than eating. For a while she settled down in South Dakota with a second husband, whom she had saved at a card game by shooting his attacker. After being widowed again, she continued her gambling career at her own saloon near Fort Meade. In 1920 she shot a drunken soldier for breaking down her door, but she was acquitted by a judge who simply wouldn't convict such a nice, gray-haired old lady. She retired to a ranch after this incident, where she died at age 79.

Florence Foster Jenkins (1868–1944)
Singer

GROWING UP IN A WEALTHY, SOCIALLY PROMINENT Pennsylvania family, Florence Foster dreamed of becoming a singer. She was prevented from pursuing this ambition by her father, who forbade her to go on the stage. With his death in 1909, however, there was no one to oppose her. Her brief marriage to Dr. Frank Jenkins had ended several years earlier. With her large inheritance and social connections, Florence was able to arrange well-attended public performances, many of them benefits for charity. The only trouble was that she was the world's worst opera singer.

Although the crowds laughed at her, they did so in an affectionate way. Jenkins was never daunted, believing absolutely in her talent. She attracted such fans as the famous singer Enrico Caruso, and critics enjoyed writing cleverly-worded reviews of her recitals. Her performances included many costume changes, including that of a Spanish coquette who tossed rose petals at the audience. On October 25, 1944, the 75-year-old Jenkins made her debut at New York City's Carnegie Hall before a full house. It was the triumph of her 32-year career. She died a month later.

Jezebel (9th century B.C.E.)
Queen

THE STORY OF JEZEBEL, THE STRONG-WILLED Phoenician princess who married Ahab, king of Israel, is told in the Old Testament books 1 and 2 Kings. A devoted worshiper of the god Baal and the goddess Asherah, she used her considerable influence over her husband, not only to convert him to her religion, but also to have it established as the official religion of Israel. The Israelite priests, especially the prophet Elijah, were opposed to this new form of worship. Jezebel became so fanatical in her promotion of the religion that she had anyone who resisted her killed or driven away. The queen was blamed for the decline of the country into corruption. She continued to wield political power after Ahab's death through her two sons, who succeeded him.

The Israelites chose an army commander named Jehu to eliminate Jezebel's male descendants and reign as the new king. When Jehu came looking for Jezebel, she remained defiant, putting on makeup, elaborately dressing her hair, and taunting him from a window. She was thrown from that window to her death and, in fulfillment of one of Elijah's prophecies, her body was attacked by dogs. Since then the name Jezebel has become synonymous with a scheming seductress.

Claudia ("Lady Bird") Johnson (1912–)
First lady, environmentalist

"LADY BIRD" TAYLOR WAS A SHY 22-YEAR-OLD FROM a wealthy Texas family when she married Lyndon Baines Johnson after a whirlwind courtship. She devoted herself to his political career as he rose through the House of Representatives and Senate to the vice-presidency and presidency, acting as confidante, spokesperson, and manager for his campaigns. While Lyndon volunteered for naval service during World War II and recovered from a heart attack in 1955, Lady Bird kept his office running efficiently. As her husband's supporter, she traveled around the United States and to more than 30 foreign countries, promoting goodwill, racial integration, and the "War on Poverty." Her skill as a hostess helped make Lyndon's transition from vice-president to president easier after the assassination of John Kennedy in 1963.

Lady Bird was also a respected activist and businessperson in her own right. She turned a failing radio station into a multimillion-dollar business and managed it along with the family ranches. The gifts to the nation for which she is best remembered are the Highway Beautification Act of 1965 and the National Wildflower Research Center, the results of her tireless work on behalf of the environment. The beautiful wildflowers seen by the side of many of the nation's highways are the product of her efforts.

Winnie Ruth Judd (1905–1998)
Murderer

WINNIE JUDD WAS LIVING IN PHOENIX, ARIZONA, in October 1931, when she shot her roommates, Agnes LeRoi and Hedvig Samuelson. Afterward she packed their bodies into a trunk and several suitcases and boarded a train with her gruesome luggage. In Los Angeles a station attendant noticed something red dripping from the trunk, and Judd was apprehended. The trial of the "trunk murderer" created a sensation. Judd claimed she'd acted in self-defense (she did have a bullet wound in her hand), but she was sentenced to hang.

The publicity surrounding the trial sparked a nationwide debate about the death penalty, and a campaign was mounted to save her. At a special hearing, Judd clapped her hands and pulled at her hair, while her parents testified that there had been insanity in their family for 125 years. She was sentenced to life in the Arizona State Mental Hospital. If she hadn't escaped seven times, she would have been considered a model patient. During her last break, Judd remained at large for almost seven years and worked as a maid for a wealthy California woman. After being captured in 1969, she was declared sane by psychiatrists. She spent two years in prison before being paroled and then maintained a low profile until her death at age 93.

Julia (39 B.C.E.–14 C.E.)
Roman princess

JULIA WAS THE ONLY CHILD OF THE ROMAN emperor Augustus. Her first marriage lasted only two years, leaving Julia a widow at age 16. She was soon married again, to her father's chief lieutenant, Marcus Vipsanius Agrippa, a stern man much her senior. They had five children, including two sons who were adopted by Augustus as his heirs. After Agrippa died in 12 B.C.E., Julia's stepmother, Livia, lobbied for her own sons from a previous marriage to be named the heirs to the throne. Augustus agreed—and he ordered the elder son, Tiberius, to divorce his wife and marry Julia. Tiberius had dearly loved his wife and resented Julia for taking her place. After the birth of a stillborn son to Julia, Tiberius went into voluntary exile in 6 B.C.E.

Julia was known for her kindness, intelligence, and witty sense of humor. However, even her strongest supporters were shocked when she began to carry on affairs so flagrantly that all of Rome knew of her scandalous behavior. Augustus ignored the rumors until he finally had to admit his daughter had gone too far. In 2 B.C.E. he banished her to the harsh island of Pandataria but later relented and moved her to a more comfortable place. After Augustus's death in 14 C.E., Tiberius became emperor and cut off Julia's allowance. She died of malnutrition.

Eliza Bowen Jumel (1775–1865)
Adventuress

AMBITIOUS BETSY BOWEN, THE DAUGHTER OF A prostitute, was born in Providence, Rhode Island, and was determined to use her beauty to escape a life of miserable poverty. In 1794 she moved to New York City, where, under the name Eliza Brown, she met Stephen Jumel, a wealthy French wine merchant. She became his mistress and, in 1804, his wife, living in a mansion on Washington Heights that is now a historic landmark.

Although they entertained lavishly and gave to charities, the Jumels found little acceptance from society because of Eliza's background. In 1815 they sailed to France. There they were popular among the impoverished aristocrats—until Eliza wore out her welcome by openly supporting Napoleon Bonaparte,

who had played a major role in depriving the upper classes of their power during the French Revolution and the years that followed. Eliza sailed alone to New York in 1825 and began to sell Stephen's property, keeping the proceeds. He eventually returned to live with her but died penniless.

In 1833 Eliza married Aaron Burr, the former vice-president of the United States, hoping to attain the social standing she so desired. It was a stormy marriage, though. They were divorced in 1836. Eliza's last years were spent as a recluse, living in an imaginary world of social glory while her mansion fell into ruin around her.

Fanya Kaplan (1890?–1918)
Would-be assassin

THE RUSSIAN REVOLUTION OF FEBRUARY 1917 led to the overthrow of the czar and the establishment of a provisional government in which many political parties shared power. There was little agreement, as each group wanted to establish its own policies. The Bolshevik party led a second revolution in October 1917, gaining complete control with Vladimir Ilyich Lenin as its leader. Some members of rival parties considered violence as a means of reclaiming power. Fanya Kaplan, a Socialist Revolutionary, believed Lenin stood in the way of true reform. Born Feiga Roitblat, she had become an anarchist at an early age. (Anarchists believe that established government prevents society from achieving true freedom.) She had remained in Russia after her family immigrated to the United States. In 1906 she had been arrested for plotting to kill a government official and sent to Siberia, where fellow prisoners taught her about socialism. The February Revolution had brought about her release after 11 years of imprisonment.

Fearing for his life, Lenin seldom went out in public, and then only with an armed guard. On August 30, 1918, he went to an industrial plant to deliver a speech to the workers. As he was leaving, Kaplan approached and shot him in the neck. Arrested by the secret police, she was interrogated but refused to name any accomplices. She was shot in the back without receiving a trial. Against all the odds, Lenin recovered from his wounds, and his survival only increased his popularity with his followers.

Grace Kelly (1929–1982)
Princess of Monaco, actress

GRACE KELLY WAS BORN INTO A PROMINENT Philadelphia family. She worked as a photographer's model to pay for training as an actor in New York City. Her Broadway debut in 1949 was followed by roles in television dramas and a small, unnoticed movie appearance. It was her performance opposite Gary Cooper in *High Noon* (1952) that captured audiences' attention. Her talent and her beauty—which was described as cool, elegant, and sensual— quickly attracted ardent admirers. During her short film career, she appeared in three Alfred Hitchcock thrillers and won an Academy Award for *The Country Girl* (1954).

Kelly was filming Hitchcock's *To Catch a Thief* when she met Prince Rainier III of Monaco in 1955. Their marriage the following year was one of the biggest media events of the day. Her fans were disappointed that she never returned to acting but thrilled that their idol had become a genuine princess. She devoted herself to the people of Monaco, charity work, cultural activities, and raising three children. The real-life fairy tale ended in tragedy when her car plunged off a winding road and she was fatally injured in the crash.

Constance Kent (1844–?)
Murderer

ON JUNE 29, 1860, A THREE-YEAR-OLD BOY WAS found dead, his throat brutally slashed, on the grounds of his family's estate in the English countryside. Scotland Yard investigator Jonathan Whicher soon named 16-year-old Constance Kent, the boy's half sister, as a suspect in the murder. Victorian society was greatly shocked. Constance appeared to be a proper upper-class girl, well-mannered, pretty, and respectful. However, as Whicher had discovered, she was also bitterly resentful of her father's second wife and the children he had with her. Whicher could produce no evidence of his suspicions, thanks to the bumbling of the local police, who had arrived first on the scene. Constance herself coolly denied responsibility. When the investigator had the girl arrested and tried for the murder, public opinion turned so strongly against him that his career was ruined. She was declared innocent and released.

Constance entered a French convent and later moved to a religious retreat in England. There she was prompted, unexpectedly, to confess that she had committed the crime after all. At her sensational trial in 1865, she was condemned to death, although the sentence was changed to life imprisonment in consideration of her youth. She was released 20 years later and disappeared into obscurity.

Ilse Koch (1906–1967)
Sadist, war criminal

THE NAZI STORM TROOPERS WERE HER IDOLS, AND Ilse Koch was determined to share their power. She had achieved this goal in 1936, when she married Colonel Karl Koch. The colonel soon became commandant of the Buchenwald concentration camp, where 55,000 people would die. Although her husband was convicted of embezzlement and executed by his superiors in 1945, Ilse stayed at Buchenwald until she was arrested by American troops at the end of World War II.

Appearing before the war crimes tribunal in Nuremburg, Koch claimed she was a simple housewife and mother, unaware of the atrocities around her. However, eyewitnesses testified she had been the instigator of horrifying acts, including the torture and murder of dozens of prisoners. Her most perverse crime was to have prisoners killed and their skins made into lampshades, book covers, and gloves. The Nuremberg judges gave her a life sentence, but in 1949, despite worldwide protests, Koch was released, only to be arrested immediately by the German police. Sentenced a second time to life in prison, she eventually hanged herself with her bedsheets.

Marie Fortunée Cappelle Lafarge (1816–1852)

Poisoner

IT WAS A MARRIAGE DOOMED FROM THE START: THE bride, Marie Cappelle, was well-educated, cultured, and socially ambitious. The groom, Charles Lafarge, was coarse and ill-bred. He had pretended to be the owner of a prosperous ironworks and a beautiful castle in the south of France. The truth—as Marie discovered after leaving her glamorous life in Paris—was that his business was failing and his castle was a dilapidated ruin. Instead of abandoning the marriage—and suing the matrimonial agency that had brokered the match—Marie bought arsenic, telling the druggist that she wanted to kill the rats plaguing her new home. She then baked a cake for her husband, who promptly fell ill. Under Marie's seemingly tender care, his condition worsened. By the time the suspicious household alerted the authorities, Lafarge was dead.

Marie's murder trial sparked sensation and controversy throughout France in 1840. Many sided with the beautiful widow. Her defense attorney, Charles Lachaud, fell in love with her. Perhaps the most notable aspect of the case was that its verdict was among the first ever based on the report of a toxicologist, or scientist specializing in poisons. Dr. Mathieu Orfila's discovery of arsenic in Lafarge's body condemned Marie to life imprisonment. In 1852 Emperor Napoleon III released her because she was suffering from advanced tuberculosis. She died soon after.

Jeanne de Valois, Comtesse de La Motte (1756–1791)

Swindler

IN 1782 COMTESSE JEANNE DE LA MOTTE ARRIVED in Paris with her husband. Although she was descended from a French king's illegitimate son, her family had been reduced to poverty, and she lived on handouts from friends. She dreamed of regaining the riches she felt she deserved, but her appeals to King Louis XVI fell on deaf ears. The small pension she was granted was not enough to support the grand lifestyle she desired, so she turned to swindling. Her schemes were bold, but perhaps not clever enough to

The Plot

Jeanne approached Cardinal de Rohan, a nobleman who had fallen out of favor with the queen, and promised to help him regain her friendship. Later she told Rohan that Marie-Antoinette wished him to negotiate the purchase of the diamond necklace, which he did, arranging for the queen to pay in installments. Once Jeanne had the necklace, she began selling off the stones. She sent Rohan letters from the queen, later proved to be poor forgeries, and staged a meeting at which the queen was impersonated by a streetwalker. The scandal broke when the first installment came due and the queen refused to pay.

be brilliant. She was responsible for the "Affair of the Diamond Necklace," which would become a favorite literary subject.

The affair's convoluted plot involved a fabulous diamond necklace, a powerful nobleman who was used as a dupe, forged letters, impersonations, and possibly Queen Marie-Antoinette's cooperation. At the end of the sensational trial, Jeanne was punished with a public branding and imprisonment. However, she escaped after nine months and fled to England, where she published her highly unreliable memoirs. She died when she tried to escape her creditors by jumping out of a window.

For years speculation continued over whether Marie-Antoinette really had been involved in the diamond necklace swindle. The story was used as an example of her corruption and extravagance when the French monarchy was finally overthrown in 1792.

Marie Laveau (1790?–1881)

Voodoo priestess

IN THE 1820S MARIE LAVEAU ACHIEVED NOTORIETY as the "Voodoo Queen of New Orleans" through a combination of dramatic flair, clever business sense, and ruthless power-grabbing. Laveau recognized the potential profit in the sensational aspects of voodoo, or *voudun*, a religion with African roots that evolved among slaves in Haiti before arriving in Louisiana. She publicized the rituals conducted in New Orleans and demanded admission fees from white people who came seeking thrills. She drove other voudun practitioners, potential competitors, out of town. She also made use of secrets she learned while working as a hairdresser in wealthy homes. Playing upon peoples' superstitions, Laveau made a small fortune selling "magic" potions, spells, and prophecies, while inspiring fearful obedience in people of all classes. At the same time, Laveau, a mulatto (a person of mixed white and black ancestry), was a respected leader in the black community, conducting authentic voudun services in private, tirelessly nursing invalids, and comforting prisoners.

One of Laveau's 15 children was a daughter who took over her mother's role—and her name—when the older woman retired in 1875. The two Maries looked so similar that many people, unaware of the daughter's existence, believed the mother had magically preserved her youth. The second Marie disappeared after her mother died in 1881. More than one tomb in New Orleans is said to belong to Laveau; believers still visit them in search of supernatural aid.

Lolita Lebrón is led away by the police after the shooting.

Lolita Lebrón (1920–)
Nationalist, terrorist

A T THE END OF THE SPANISH AMERICAN WAR IN 1898, Puerto Rico came under American control. Many Puerto Ricans were in favor of commonwealth status (the situation that exists now), in which the island holds wide powers of self-rule but maintains a voluntary association with the United States. Others wanted their island nation to become the 51st state; still others desired complete independence. One of those who most ardently sought independence was Lolita Lebrón, a Puerto Rican woman who had come to New York in 1940 to work in the garment industry. While her two children were raised by her family back home, Lebrón became involved in union organization and political activism.

On March 1, 1954, Lebrón led three Puerto Rican men into the visitors' gallery of the House of Representatives in Washington, D.C. She unfolded a Puerto Rican flag and waved it to gain the attention of the congressmen on the floor below; she then took a gun from her purse and fired. She and her companions, who also fired shots, wounded five congressmen before they were arrested. They were given 75-year prison sentences but were released by President Jimmy Carter in 1979. Lebrón returned to Puerto Rico, where she was welcomed as a heroine rather than a terrorist. She continues to crusade for independence, although she now supports nonviolence.

Gypsy Rose Lee (1914–1970)
Burlesque star, writer

G YPSY ROSE LEE WAS THE FIRST BURLESQUE dancer to bring wit and sophistication to the art of the striptease. Her performances were self-aware and ironic; she offered a humorous commentary on American attitudes toward sex and

Ida Lewis (1842–1911)

Lighthouse keeper

IDA LEWIS BEGAN HER CAREER AS KEEPER OF THE Lime Rock Lighthouse in Newport Harbor, Rhode Island, in 1857. Her father, the official keeper, had suffered a stroke, so she took over his duties. During her almost 50 years as keeper, she not only tended the light but also saved at least 22 people and one prizewinning sheep from drowning.

Ida came to national attention in 1869, when a journalist from *Harper's Magazine* reported that she had rowed half a mile in freezing March weather without a hat, coat, or shoes to rescue two soldiers. As a result, visitors flocked to Newport to see her. The community showered her with gifts, and she received a Congressional Medal of Honor. Men, some of whom she'd never met, begged to marry her. She did marry a sailor, but they soon separated. All the attention was difficult for Ida, who valued her privacy. In 1879 the government finally made her the official keeper of the lighthouse she'd been tending for 20 years. She remained at her post until the age of 77, when she suffered a fatal stroke.

managed to be suggestive without sacrificing her dignity. She was also known for her intellectual reading habits, clever sayings, and outspokenness on legal and political matters.

Born Rose Louise Hovick, she made her stage debut at the age of four. Under the guidance of her ruthless but charming mother, Madam Rose, Gypsy and her sister, June (who became famous as June Havoc), joined the vaudeville circuit. The girls never went to school, although Gypsy became self-educated. In Kansas City, at age 15, she stepped into her first solo strip act, having learned the trade from Tessie the Tassel Twirler. She shot to stardom, appearing on Broadway at Billy Minsky's Republic Theatre and with the Ziegfeld Follies. In an attempt to clean up the city, Mayor Fiorello La Guardia closed New York's burlesque houses in 1942. After that Lee went to Hollywood, where she appeared in films and musicals, at nightclubs, and on television. A talented writer, she published articles, thrillers such as *The Naked Genius* (1943), and an autobiography, *Gypsy* (1957), which became a musical on stage and screen.

Lozen (1848?–1890?)

Apache warrior

DURING THE EARLY 1870S, THE UNITED STATES government forced the Apache Indians to move to reservations, giving up their homeland, which included parts of Mexico, New Mexico, and Arizona. In 1877 a group of Warm Springs Apaches fled their reservation in Arizona, determined to fight in order to return to their traditional way of life. Among them was Lozen, the only known Apache woman warrior. She won the admiration of her people with her courage and abilities with horses and weapons. Skilled in strategy, she was invited to sit on war councils. Lozen had an uncanny ability to detect the enemy's whereabouts, which was credited to supernatural powers.

Lozen's band of "rebels," led by her kinsman Victorio, was hunted by both the American and Mexican armies. After Victorio's death she joined the last band of free Apaches and gained the respect of their leader Geronimo. Forced to surrender in 1886, the Apache warriors were sent to military barracks in Alabama. The conditions were so terrible that starvation and disease killed most of the captives, including Lozen, the woman who had braved so many bullets.

Zivia Lubetkin (1914–1976)
Resistance fighter

WHEN THE GERMAN ARMY INVADED POLAND IN September 1939, Zivia Lubetkin was in Geneva, Switzerland, where she had been serving as a delegate to the Zionist Congress. (Zionists supported the establishment of an independent Jewish community in Palestine.) She chose to return to her native Poland to help defend her people. She served as a message courier and arms smuggler for the Jewish underground resistance movement based in the ghetto of occupied Warsaw. As the mass deportation of Jews began in 1942, she helped found the Zydowska Organizacja Bojowa (Jewish Fighting Organization) and played an important role as a member of the political committee and the only woman commander. Lubetkin was among those Polish Jews who first offered armed resistance against the Nazis in January 1943, and she fought in the Warsaw Ghetto Uprising a few months later. Fleeing through the sewers to the non-Jewish part of the city, she continued her resistance activities, participating in the Warsaw Uprising of 1944.

Among wartime resistance groups, "Zivia" soon became a code word for Poland. After the country was liberated, Lubetkin helped to bring Holocaust survivors to Palestine. In 1947 she and her husband, fellow resistance fighter Yitzhak Zuckerman, settled in the Jewish homeland and cofounded a kibbutz, or cooperative farming community. They returned to Europe in 1961 to testify in the war crimes trial of Adolf Eichmann.

Sybil Ludington (1761–1839)
Patriot

PAUL REVERE WAS NOT THE ONLY AMERICAN patriot to make a daring midnight ride to call the colonists to arms against the British. Sybil Ludington rode twice as far as her male counterpart, but she has gotten much less attention.

Sybil was the daughter of Henry Ludington, a militia colonel in the Revolutionary War. On the night of April 26, 1777, an exhausted messenger reached the Ludington house in Fredericksburg, New York, with word that the British were attacking Danbury, just over the Connecticut border. Since the region's munitions and supplies were stored there, the revolutionaries had to take immediate action. Sixteen-year-old Sybil volunteered to ride out and alert her father's troops. She traveled 40 miles (64 km) over rough terrain, calling together armed volunteers who assembled by dawn the next day. The patriots were unable to save Danbury, but the redcoats were forced to retreat and suffered serious losses. Sybil's hometown was renamed Ludingtonville in her honor.

Sophie Levy Lyons (1848–1924)
Swindler, gossip columnist

AS SOON AS SOPHIE LEVY COULD WALK, HER parents introduced her to their way of life: shoplifting and picking pockets on the streets of New York City. The future "Queen of Crime" was audacious, clever, and beautiful. She impressed her criminal mentors, including the notorious thief Ned Lyons, who became the second of her three husbands. Their tumultuous relationship endured through an outrageous double-escape from Sing Sing prison, disagreements over whether they should give up the thieving life, and the birth of four children. Sophie was imprisoned many times, but she also frequently evaded arrest with Oscar-worthy performances of wronged innocence.

During the 1880s Sophie lived in Europe, masterminding one sensational heist after another. She amassed a fortune, which allowed her to acquire the education in arts, culture, and language necessary to join high society. Her wealthy new friends accepted

her as one of their own, never suspecting that she was responsible when their jewels disappeared. Back in the United States, Sophie turned to blackmail and the more legitimate profession of investing in real estate. In the 1890s she retired from crime, settled in Detroit, and set about reforming other criminals. She also became America's first gossip columnist, using her social connections to gather interesting tidbits for the *New York World* newspaper. Ironically Sophie was beaten to death during a burglary by some of the criminals she sought to reform.

Sharon Christa McAuliffe (1948–1986)
Teacher, astronaut

CHRISTA MCAULIFFE WAS A HIGH SCHOOL SOCIAL studies teacher and mother of two when the National Aeronautics and Space Administration (NASA) chose her from 11,000 applicants to be the first private citizen in space. In 1985 the dynamic, dedicated teacher left her home in Concord, New Hampshire, to begin five months of training at the Johnson Space Center in Houston. She made plans to

document her adventure, provide lessons from space to classrooms around the world via satellite, and lecture on her experience when she returned.

As the time approached for the launch, problems arose, including a severe cold front that left ice on the launchpad at Kennedy Space Center in Cape Canaveral, Florida. After several delays, the space shuttle *Challenger* was finally ready to lift off on January 28, 1986. McAuliffe and her six crewmates prepared themselves. Family and friends watched from the ground, and millions of viewers watched on television as the *Challenger* launched at 11:38 A.M. Seventy-three seconds later, it burst into flames, killing everyone onboard. NASA had hoped to revive public interest in its programs by taking a private citizen into space, but the tragedy damaged its reputation and halted shuttle missions for almost three years.

Oseola McCarty (1908–1999)
Philanthropist

BORN INTO A POOR FAMILY IN WAYNE COUNTY, Mississippi, Oseola McCarty left school and began working as a laundress at age 12. She worked tirelessly, never marrying or having children, never owning a car or indulging in other luxuries. She began putting money into a savings account, where it accumulated until the employees at her local bank encouraged her to invest it in accounts that earned higher interest. It eventually grew to about $250,000.

In 1994, at the age of 87, McCarty's arthritis forced her to retire from washing and ironing. She decided to set aside some of her savings for living expenses, to earmark some for church and family members, and the rest—60 percent of the total—she donated to the University of Southern Mississippi. Although she had never visited the college in her hometown of Hattiesburg, she knew the importance of education and wanted to establish a scholarship to help young, financially needy African American students. Her astounding act of generosity inspired many others to contribute to the university. It also generated media attention and more than 150 awards for McCarty, including the Presidential Citizens Medal, a high civilian honor. Despite the hoopla, McCarty continued to live modestly, walking to the store and only turning on the air conditioner when company came.

Flora Macdonald (1722–1790)
Patriot

IN 1745 CHARLES EDWARD STUART—BONNIE Prince Charlie—began his campaign to reclaim the British throne lost by his grandfather, King James II, 57 years earlier. In Scotland the prince rallied the Highland clans to his cause, but his troops were defeated at the Battle of Culloden, and he became a fugitive. Flora Macdonald was asked to help him escape. Despite the danger of discovery, Flora ferried Prince Charles, who had been disguised as a maid, to her mother's home on the Isle of Skye. He took shelter there before escaping to France. When word got out, Flora was arrested and imprisoned in the Tower of London, although her bravery made her a celebrity. Soon released, she returned home and married Allan Macdonald.

English persecution of the Highlanders increased after the rebellion. In 1774 the Macdonalds immigrated to North Carolina, where they prospered. Unfortunately the outbreak of the Revolutionary War raised a dilemma for Flora and other Scots: Should they support the English, who had treated them harshly back home, or the American patriots? In the end they sided with the loyalists. Allan became a colonel and was captured by the patriots. Their property was confiscated. Flora sailed for Scotland. On the way her ship was attacked by a French privateer, but she survived. She was eventually reunited with her husband on Skye, where she spent her last years.

Malintzin (La Malinche) (1500?–1530?)
Adviser to Hernán Cortés

TO SOME, SHE WAS A HEROINE, TO OTHERS, A traitor. In saving her people from the domination of the Aztec empire, Malintzin opened the door to the Spanish conquest of Mexico. The daughter of a village chieftain, she was born in what is now the Veracruz region. She grew up privileged but was sold into slavery by her stepmother. As a slave, she was valued for her intelligence, aptitude for languages, and beauty. Hoping to appease the Spanish with gifts, her owners gave her to Hernán Cortés when he arrived in 1519. As it turned out, she became Cortés's adviser, interpreter, guide, and nurse, a valuable asset in his campaign to conquer the land and convert the Mexican people to Christianity.

Malintzin was christened Doña Marina, although she is better known by the Spanish adaptation of her native name, La Malinche. She accompanied Cortés on his expeditions, encouraging him to negotiate with the native people rather than simply slaughter them. But she also assisted with strategy in his battles against the Aztec ruler, Montezuma. By the time the Aztec empire fell, La Malinche was pregnant with Cortés's son. This boy, born in 1522, was one of the very first *mestizos*, the people of mixed Spanish and Indian blood who make up the majority of the Mexican population today. To them, La Malinche is the "Mexican Eve."

Mary Mallon (1870?–1938)
Disease carrier

IN THE EARLY 1900s, THE NEW YORK CITY AREA suffered a severe outbreak of typhoid fever. The disease reached epidemic proportions, claiming hundreds of lives. Finally George Soper, a sanitary engineer at the New York City Department of Health, found a common factor in the households identified as sources of the fever: the cook, an Irish American immigrant named Mary Mallon. Each time Mary took a job, her employers would fall ill. She would then move on to a new post, not realizing that she brought infection with her wherever she went.

At the time scientists did not yet know that typhoid could be carried and spread by people such as Mary, who were themselves immune. Soper proved this in 1907 when he tested Mary for infection. The press dubbed her "Typhoid Mary," and because she refused to stop cooking, she was committed to an isolation hospital for three years. Released on condition that she not endanger others by handling food, Mary soon escaped health department surveillance and went back to the work she loved best. Twenty-five employees at a Manhattan maternity hospital got sick in 1915, and Mary was again the cause. She was forced to return to the isolation hospital, where she spent the rest of her life.

Fredericka "Marm" Mandelbaum (1819?–1894)
Fence

FREDERICKA MANDELBAUM, BETTER KNOWN AS "Marm," immigrated to New York City from Prussia and became one of the most sociable and notorious criminals of the 19th century. She sold goods stolen by the country's top thieves in a fencing operation so large and well-planned that she became a millionaire and evaded arrest for 30 years. She also turned her brownstone townhouse into a school for crime. There she trained burglars, swindlers, pickpockets, safecrackers, and blackmailers. Many of her apprentices were female. She also held elaborate dinner parties that were attended not only by her criminal friends, but also by politicians and judges.

In 1884 Manhattan district attorney Peter Olney joined forces with the Pinkerton detective agency to plan a raid on Marm's headquarters. Upon discovering art, antiques, and jewels worth a king's ransom stashed in the brownstone, they arrested her. Aided by her clever lawyers, Mandelbaum escaped to Canada with more than enough of her ill-gotten riches to retire in comfort. It is said that she visited New York City several times in disguise and that her body was brought back there for burial.

Imelda Marcos (1930–)
First lady of the Philippines

BEAUTY CONTEST–WINNER IMELDA ROMUALDEZ married rising politician Ferdinand Marcos, who became president of the Philippines in 1965. She gained power as the leader of her own political faction and as her husband's ambassador and diplomatic negotiator. She was elected to—or given—several important government positions. She also made herself an international celebrity, socializing with film stars and performing pop songs at political rallies. Throughout their time in office, the Marcoses were accused of corruption, including election fraud and human rights abuse. While many Filipinos suffered in poverty, the Marcoses lived in luxury and spent government resources on wasteful building projects.

Ferdinand's health began to fail in 1983, and a nonviolent revolution swept him from office in 1986. Imelda fled with her husband and entourage to Hawaii, leaving behind her infamous legacy: thousands of pairs of shoes and other proofs of her spending habits. Marcos died in 1989, and Imelda faced major legal battles over the money he was accused of stealing from his country. She stood trial in the United States and in her home country (she returned in 1991) but managed to escape jail. In fact, she launched a comeback political campaign and was elected to the Philippine house of representatives in 1995. Imelda continues to buy shoes and claims she only did what was best for her country.

Marie-Antoinette (1755–1793)
Queen of France

MARIE-ANTOINETTE, THE 11TH DAUGHTER OF Maria Theresa and Holy Roman Emperor Francis I, was married at age 15 to the French dauphin (the eldest son of the king). The royal bride

found her husband uninteresting and uninterested in her. By the time he became King Louis XVI in 1774, she was spending all her time with a group of dissolute court favorites. She became notorious for her extravagant spending and rumored love affairs. Royal scandals, especially the "Affair of the Diamond Necklace" (perpetrated by noblewoman Jeanne de La Motte), contributed to growing dissatisfaction with the monarchy. Historians doubt that Marie-Antoinette said "Let them eat cake" after being told that the peasants had no bread, but this famous legend appears to express accurately her lack of sympathy for the poor. She gained great influence over her indecisive husband and convinced him to reject reforms sought by the National Assembly in 1789.

That year the revolutionaries took the royal family hostage. An attempt to escape failed. Efforts were made to negotiate a compromise that would implement a constitution while restoring some power to the king. These ended when Marie-Antoinette engaged in intrigues with her Austrian relatives, asking for military support at a time when France was on the brink of war with Austria. In August 1792 the monarchy was overthrown, and the following year the king and queen stood trial for treason. Both were sent to the guillotine.

Mary (late 1st century B.C.E.– early 1st century C.E.)
Mother of Jesus

WHAT WE KNOW OF MARY MUST BE DRAWN from the Bible's New Testament and other Christian writings. Born in Galilee to Jewish parents, she was engaged to Joseph, a carpenter from Nazareth, who was many years her senior and a descendant of King David. The Gospels recount that an angel warned Mary that she would conceive the son of God while remaining a virgin. When she returned from a visit with her cousin Elizabeth visibly pregnant, Joseph at first rejected her. He agreed to marry her after the angel explained the pregnancy's divine origin. The couple traveled to Bethlehem, where Mary gave birth to Jesus. The family was forced to flee to Egypt but later returned and settled in Nazareth. Mary appears in accounts of other important occasions in Jesus' life, including his crucifixion.

The story of Mary, the woman, has long since been eclipsed by the story of Mary, the holy mother.

As the worship of Jesus grew in popularity, so did a reverence for his mother, especially in the Catholic and Orthodox churches. The object of pilgrimages and visions, she is considered the embodiment of gentleness, inner strength, faith, and hope.

Mata Hari (1876–1917)
Spy

MARGARETHA ZELLE GREW UP IN THE Netherlands, the daughter of a well-to-do hatter. At age 18 she married a dashing Dutch colonial army officer, Captain MacLeod, who took her to live in Java and Sumatra. Disappointed with the hot, rainy climate and her abusive husband, she returned to Europe, obtained a divorce, and used the settlement to pay for dancing lessons. In 1905, after struggling for two years, she finally rose to stardom as an exotic dancer under a new name: Mata Hari. Showered with fame and fortune, Mata Hari took many lovers, most of them military officers, diplomats, and aristocrats. Then in 1912 she became a spy for the Germans under the direction of one of her lovers, the Berlin police chief.

It's unknown just how much military information Mata Hari—operating as secret agent H.21— gathered before and during World War I. Some say that her intelligence work led to the crushing defeat of the French at the Battle of the Somme. Others say she was too inept as a spy to do much harm. By 1917

her physical charms were fading, her espionage services were less sought-after, and the French were highly suspicious. She was arrested in Paris, tried by a military court, and sentenced to death, although she claimed she had worked for the Germans as a courtesan, not a spy, and that she had been a counterintelligence agent for the French. She went before the firing squad with courage and style.

Ulrike Meinhof (1934–1976)
Terrorist

At the end of World War II, a defeated Germany was split into two countries. East Germany, under the guidance of the Soviet Union, adopted communism, while West Germany struggled to recover from economic devastation with the help of the pro-capitalist United States. Ulrike Meinhof, who was a teenager when her country was divided, grew up in the middle of the Cold War, the state of rivalry and distrust between communist and capitalist nations. Although her middle-class family was West German, she became a political activist with strong anticapitalist views while in college. She expressed her beliefs as

editor of *Konkret* (Concrete), a student newspaper, and as a journalist for magazines, radio, and television. She married *Konkret*'s publisher, Klaus Rainer Röhl, and had twin daughters in 1962.

By the early 1970s, Meinhof had left her husband and become involved in more violent forms of protest against capitalism. She helped fellow activist Andreas Baader escape from prison, and they formed the "Red Army Faction," a paramilitary terrorist group that became known as the "Baader-Meinhof Gang." With help from the communist regime in East Germany, the gang conducted kidnappings, murders, robberies, and bombings. Among the activities in which Meinhof played a part was the 1972 bombing of Springer Press. She was captured later that year, but her trial was delayed while a specially protected courthouse was prepared. Before the construction was finished, however, Meinhof committed suicide by hanging herself.

Anne Josephe Théroigne de Méricourt (1762–1817)
Revolutionary, feminist

Born into poverty in Lièges, Belgium, Anne Josephe Méricourt found wealth and success as Théroigne de Méricourt, a singer and courtesan in London, Paris, and Italy. When revolution broke out in France in 1789, she traveled to Paris and committed herself to the cause. An ardent, pioneering feminist as well as a radical antimonarchist, Méricourt gave all her wealth to revolutionary societies and women's

> "Fellow women citizens, why should we not enter into rivalry with the men? Do they alone lay claim to have rights to glory; no, no. . . . generous fellow women citizens, all of you who hear me, let us take up arms, let us go and drill two or three times a week on the Champs Elysées, or on the Champ de la Fédération; let us open a list of French Amazons; and let all those who truly love their Fatherland write their names there. . ."
>
> Théroigne de Méricourt
> speech delivered March 1792

51

organizations. She made fiery speeches and wrote newspaper articles, advocating such measures as forming armies of women warriors. She was in the front lines at the storming of the Bastille, dressed as an Amazon. She led the Women's March on Versailles and took part in the assault on the Tuileries palace that helped bring down the monarchy.

Eventually, though, Méricourt joined forces with the moderate Girondists and lost the support of the people she was trying to liberate. While making a speech in 1793, she was attacked by a violent mob of women. The incident precipitated a mental breakdown from which she never recovered. Méricourt spent the last 20 years of her life in La Salpêtrière, an insane asylum.

Asunta Adelaide Luigia ("Tina") Modotti (1896–1942)
Photographer, spy

TINA MODOTTI WAS ASSOCIATED WITH MANY famous men, but she achieved renown in her own right as a talented photographer. As a young Italian immigrant, she found work in Hollywood as a minor stage and silent film actress, thanks to her remarkable beauty. She married artist Robo Richey and, after his death, traveled to Mexico City with photographer Edward Weston. She was Weston's model and muse; he was her mentor in the art of photography. Struck by the poverty and oppression she witnessed, Modotti joined the Mexican Communist party in 1927. Her photographs took on an increasingly political tone. She eventually gave up her art and devoted herself to espionage work for the Comintern, a Soviet organization dedicated to promoting communism worldwide.

The increasingly anti-Communist mood in Mexico led to false accusations of Modotti's involvement in two assassination plots, and in 1929 she fled to Moscow. When the Spanish Civil War broke out, she served as a nurse for the International Brigades fighting General Francisco Franco. It was during this period that she may have inspired the character of Maria in Ernest Hemingway's novel *For Whom the Bell Tolls* (1940). She returned to Mexico but died soon after, reportedly of a heart attack—although it was rumored that she had decided to leave the Communist party and had been killed to protect Comintern secrets.

Lola Montez (1818–1861)
Adventuress, dancer

LOLA MONTEZ CONSTANTLY REINVENTED HER LIFE story. In her favorite version, she was the daughter of a Spanish matador. In reality Maria Dolores Eliza Rosanna Gilbert was born in Ireland to British parents and raised in India as the spoiled darling of her father's military regiment. In the course of her sensational career, Lola traveled widely in Europe, America, and Australia, never staying in one place for long, earning fortunes and spending them, smoking cigars, cracking whips, and collecting a menagerie of animals. She was famous for her beauty, charm, and hot temper—but not her talent as a dancer, although audiences flocked to see her Spanish-style "Spider Dance." Lola lived in royal palaces and the rugged gold rush mining camps of California. She was drawn into politics through associations with intellectuals, politicians, and aristocrats.

Always at the center of a stormy scandal, Montez captivated composer Franz Liszt, author Alexandre Dumas *père*, and at least three husbands.

Lola's greatest conquest was King Ludwig I of Bavaria, who made her Countess of Landsfeld and listened devotedly to her advice on liberal reform. Her control of the elderly king was a catalyst for the revolution in Bavaria and Ludwig's eventual abdication. In the last years of her life, a penitent Montez lived in New York City, where she lectured on womanhood and withdrew into spiritualism and religion.

Evelyn Nesbit (1884–1967)

Chorus girl

EVELYN NESBIT WAS 16 YEARS OLD, IMPOVERISHED, and startlingly beautiful when she and her widowed mother moved from Pittsburgh to New York City. Their fortunes improved as Evelyn found work as a model and chorus girl. She attracted the attention of Stanford White, one of the most successful architects of the era as well as a connoisseur of beautiful girls. Soon White was supporting Nesbit financially, providing her with an education, and introducing her to high society.

Nesbit, however, was in the market for a rich husband, and since White was already married, she settled on Harry Thaw. The heir to millions, he was known as "Mad Harry" for his wild behavior. Thaw became obsessed with his fiancée's earlier relationship with White, and he often beat her in a jealous rage. Despite his cruelty Nesbit married Thaw in 1905. His fury continued to escalate until the night of June 25, 1906, when Thaw shot and killed White. The event was all the more shocking because it happened in full view of New York's fashionable society, at the rooftop theater of Madison Square Garden, which White had designed. Thaw was found innocent by reason of insanity and institutionalized for eight years. Nesbit went on to perform in vaudeville, drawing audiences curious to see the woman who had inspired such a sensational murder. Her second marriage also failed. She spent her last years in California and died at age 82.

Catherine O'Leary (?–1895)

Scapegoat

ON THE NIGHT OF OCTOBER 8, 1871, A FIRE BEGAN in a barn in a poor neighborhood on Chicago's South Side. After a hot, dry summer, in a city composed almost entirely of wooden buildings, the flames quickly raged out of control. The Great Chicago Fire lasted for 30 hours, leaping over the river, engulfing more than a quarter of the city's buildings, killing 300, leaving 100,000 homeless, and eventually bankrupting 56 insurance companies. Desperate for someone to blame, the people chose Mrs. O'Leary.

Catherine O'Leary, who lived with her husband, Patrick, and five children in a house on DeKoven Street, operated a dairy business. The fire had started in her barn. The O'Learys explained that they had gone to bed early on the night of the fire, and a thorough investigation found no truth to the rumors that arose. However, journalists latched on to the idea that Mrs. O'Leary had been milking a cow that kicked over a lamp and started the fire. Stung by the negative articles, cartoons, and songs, Catherine and her husband avoided publicity, and little more is known about them. Today a training school for firefighters stands on the site of the O'Leary house.

Grace O'Malley (1530?–1603?)

Pirate, Irish chieftain

GRACE O'MALLEY, KNOWN IN HER NATIVE GAELIC language as Gráinne ni Mhaille or Gráunuaile, was the most famous and feared of a long line of warriors and ship captains. While she was growing up on Clare Island, many Irish chieftains were forced to turn their lands over to the conquering English in return for safety and a title. The daughter of Owen Dubhdara, chieftain of Umhall Uachtarach, Grace would grow up to fight against the English and—upon occasion during times of war—to offer her services on their behalf. She would rule the lands and seas on the northwest coast of Ireland by inheritance and, more significantly, through her own bravery and skill in battle. Her two marriages brought her more lands and four children, but she remained independent and in charge. She conducted trade as far afield as Spain and demanded tolls from ships sailing the seas she controlled or simply plundered them.

O'Malley met her match in the British governor, Sir Richard Bingham. Her refusal to submit to English laws and customs or to give up her role as pirate queen landed her in prison; she would have been hanged if the chieftains of Mayo had not negotiated her release. Still Bingham's cruel tactics deprived her of her lands, ships, and followers. Undaunted, Grace went to London to appeal to Queen Elizabeth I in 1593 and was granted a pension and permission to return to the seas.

Jacqueline Bouvier Kennedy Onassis (1929–1994)
First lady, socialite

BORN INTO A WEALTHY NEW YORK FAMILY, Jacqueline Bouvier was named Debutante of the Year in 1947 and was educated at Vassar, the University of Paris, and George Washington University. After spending two years as a photographer and reporter for the *Washington Times-Herald*, she married eligible bachelor Senator John F. Kennedy in 1953. Jackie devoted herself to her husband's career and to their children, Caroline and John, Jr., both before and after Kennedy was elected

president in 1960. As first lady she captured the world's attention with her elegant style. Women copied "the Jackie look," especially her pillbox hats and simple suits. Record numbers tuned in to watch a televised tour of the White House, which Jackie had redecorated with period antiques. She became as popular as her husband, representing him as an unofficial diplomat on international visits.

This glamorous life ended in November 1963, when Kennedy was assassinated while riding with Jackie in a motorcade through Dallas, Texas. Jackie set an example for the mourning nation by courageously coping with her own grief. Her 1968 marriage to Greek shipping tycoon Aristotle Onassis came as a surprise to the public. She lived in relative seclusion until Onassis's death in 1975. Returning to New York City, she started a career as a book editor, first at Viking, then at Doubleday. She also dedicated herself to preserving historic architecture and was a key figure in saving Grand Central Station from demolition. Her death at age 64 was caused by cancer.

Bonnie Parker (1911–1934)
Outlaw

THE INFAMOUS DUO OF BONNIE AND CLYDE WAS formed in January 1930 when small-time thief Clyde Barrow met Bonnie Parker, who at age 19 was bored with her life as a café waitress in Dallas, Texas. Soon after their meeting, Clyde was arrested and Bonnie helped him escape by visiting him in jail with a gun taped to her leg. In 1932, when they were finally free to begin their life of crime together, they raided the National Guard Armory in Fort Worth for weapons and ammunition and ranged through Texas, Oklahoma, New Mexico, and Missouri, robbing banks and stores. They would have been only minor crooks—they never got away with more than $1,500—if they hadn't sought attention by sending poems about their exploits and photographs of themselves holding machine guns to the newspapers. Depression-era America was fascinated by their flamboyance and horrified by their senseless killings and shoot-outs with police. The pair claimed 15 victims in all.

With the law hot on their trail, Bonnie knew their wild spree couldn't last, but she'd had what she wanted: 21 months of fame and excitement. In the end Bonnie and Clyde were ambushed by police on a road near Gibsland, Louisiana. Clyde took 24 bullets and Bonnie, 23.

Charlotte "Charley" Parkhurst (1812?–1879)
Stagecoach driver

I N 1868 IN CALIFORNIA, CHARLEY PARKHURST voted in a presidential election. No one remarked on this momentous event at the time—but they would have, if they had known "Charley" was a woman. It would be another half century before American women won the legal right to vote.

Charlotte Parkhurst was left in a New Hampshire orphanage as a child and later escaped, wearing boys' clothes. The disguise enabled her to find work with horses, which she loved, so she never abandoned it. She became one of the most skillful stagecoach drivers in New England and, later, in California. She lost an eye when a horse kicked her in the face, and her eyepatch made discovery of her secret even less likely. Bundled in bulky clothing and wearing gloves to hide her small hands, she fearlessly drove the routes through gold-fever boomtowns and was regularly entrusted with shipments of gold. Parkhurst's sex was nearly discovered several times, but only after her death was it revealed that tough, one-eyed Charley was not a man, and had probably even given birth.

Sofya Lvovna Perovskaya (1855?–1881)
Assassin

A LTHOUGH SOFYA PEROVSKAYA CAME FROM AN aristocratic, socially prominent Russian family, she developed an opposition to her country's political system. Czar Alexander II, while attempting to enact several progressive reforms in the country, still maintained an autocratic control. Working as a teacher and nurse in St. Petersburg, Perovskaya became involved in revolutionary activities and joined the "Land and Liberty" group. That group split due to ideological differences in 1879, so she

and her lover, Andrei Zhelyabov, formed a new movement, "The People's Will," which sought to bring about political change through terrorism.

Although there had been attempts on the life of Czar Alexander II, he continued to go out in public, driving along the Nevsky Prospekt in his sleigh. In March 1881 Perovskaya stationed members of her group along the czar's route. Under her direction, bombs were thrown at the czar. The first one killed two bystanders, but the second struck its target. Zhelyabov and another conspirator named Nikolai Rysakov were captured at the murder scene. Rysakov turned informant and the other conspirators, including Perovskaya, were arrested. She and five others were hanged in Semenovsky Square while more than 100,000 people looked on in silence.

Molly Pitcher (1753?–1832)
War heroine

M ANY WOMEN FOLLOWED THEIR HUSBANDS TO battle during the Revolutionary War. Their stories may have been blended together into the legend of "Molly Pitcher." Most often one woman,

Mary (or Molly) Hays, is credited with being the original heroine. Molly's husband, William, enlisted in a Pennsylvania artillery regiment in 1777. She went with him and joined the rough army life of marching and camping, cooking and doing laundry for the troops.

It was at the 1778 Battle of Monmouth, in New Jersey, that Molly earned her nickname. The day was terribly hot. The soldiers, especially the wounded, were suffering, and the cannons needed to be kept cool in order to fire. Molly carried pitcher after pitcher of water for both men and guns. She earned a second nickname, "Sergeant Molly," when she took William's place as a gunner after he collapsed from heat and exhaustion. Bravely facing the enemy bombardment, she fired the cannon with enthusiasm.

Molly was widowed around 1788; she then married John McCauly. She was eventually awarded a government pension for her service on the battlefield, and her grave in Carlisle, Pennsylvania, bears a monument to her bravery.

Etta Place (1880?–after 1908)
Outlaw

ETTA PLACE'S CHILDHOOD AND EARLY YEARS ARE A mystery. Her story begins around 1897, when she joined the legendary Butch Cassidy and the Sundance Kid and their "Wild Bunch"—a gang of outlaws who ranged through the Old West robbing trains and banks and stealing cattle. Not much is known about the adventure-loving woman who rode with them, except that she was unusually beautiful, black-haired, and might have been a schoolteacher before turning to crime. She was romantically attached to the Sundance Kid (whose real name was Harry Longabaugh), the best shot in the group. She went with him and Cassidy when they fled to South America about 1901. There she helped them commit bank robberies by "casing the joints" while pretending to open accounts.

In 1907 Place and the Sundance Kid returned to the United States. She had surgery for appendicitis in New York City and then went to Denver to recuperate. The Kid rejoined Cassidy in South America, where according to many sources, they were soon killed. However, persistent rumors claim that they survived and even that Etta and the Kid were eventually reunited. Either way, the end of her story is as uncertain as the beginning.

Pocahontas (1595?–1617)
Native American heroine

POCAHONTAS WAS THE DAUGHTER OF POWHATAN, chief of the 30-tribe Algonquin confederacy in the area where the English established the colony of Jamestown, Virginia, in 1607. That year 12-year-old Pocahontas persuaded her father to save the life of Captain John Smith, who had been taken prisoner. This was the beginning of Pocahontas's role as peacemaker. With her cheerful nature, she made friends easily with the struggling settlers; she brought them gifts of food and encouraged trade. After Smith returned to England in 1609, relations worsened. Pocahontas was taken prisoner by the English in 1613. However, while in captivity, she was treated with respect. She was baptized a Christian under the name "Rebecca," and she married an influential tobacco grower named John Rolfe. Chief Powhatan ransomed his daughter and gave the couple land. The peace that was brought about by the union lasted nearly a decade.

In 1616, accompanied by her husband, their son, and several members of her tribe, Pocahontas traveled to England, where she won popularity and was presented to King James I. She fell ill during the cold, wet English winter and died just before she was to return home. During the 18th century, novels, poetry, and plays inspired by Pocahontas's life gave rise to such legends as the idea she was romantically involved with John Smith.

Diane de Poitiers (1499–1566)

Mistress of the king of France

In 1531 two events occurred in the life of beautiful, lively Diane de Poitiers: Her husband, Louis de Brézé, Comte de Maulevrier, died, and 17-year-old Prince Henry, heir to the throne of France and 20 years her junior, fell madly in love with her. Diane had received the sort of upbringing usually reserved for boys. She had been well-educated and encouraged to ride and hunt. She had come to the French court as a lady-in-waiting, first to the mother of King Francis I, then to his wife. Encouraged by the king, de Poitiers became Henry's mistress and the dominant influence in his life throughout his reign, which lasted from 1547 to 1559.

Although she ruled beside Henry as virtual queen, Diane was less interested in affairs of state than in her patronage of the arts and in using her power to accumulate privileges for her family and favorites. The friend of poets and artists, she represented the height of culture for her era. Despite her unconventional role, she was quite traditional. She always wore proper widow's black and led the conservative Catholic faction at court. After Henry's death, his wife, Catherine de Médicis, who had been forced to live in the background all this time, made Diane return the wealth Henry had bestowed upon her and retire to her château at Anet.

Haviva Reik (1914–1944)

Resistance fighter

Born in a village near Banská Bystrica, Slovakia, Haviva Reik joined the Zionist movement as a young girl and helped other Jews immigrate to Palestine, where she herself moved in 1939. She lived on a kibbutz (communal farm) until she learned of the horrors perpetrated by the Nazis in Europe and decided to aid the resistance efforts of fellow Jews still in Europe. Enlisting in the underground Jewish military organization, the Haganah, she volunteered to join a parachute unit in a mission run by the British.

The British authorities refused to send a woman behind enemy lines, so Reik joined up with some American pilots and dropped by parachute into Slovakia in September 1944. She landed in familiar territory near Banská Bystrica and met the other volunteers who had parachuted in. Joining forces with leaders in the Slovak uprising, they organized relief for refugees, helped Jewish children escape, and rescued Allied POWs. They spent much of their time simply fighting for their lives. After a month the Germans occupied the town, and Reik escaped with a group of partisans to a camp in the mountains. There they were captured by Ukrainian Nazi troops, and after interrogation and torture Reik was executed by firing squad.

Ethel Greenglass Rosenberg (1915–1953)

Suspected spy

Ethel Greenglass, the daughter of Jewish immigrants to New York City's Lower East Side, became involved in left-wing politics while working as a secretary. In 1939 she married fellow Communist party–member Julius Rosenberg, who

Ethel and Julius Rosenberg

became a civilian engineer with the U.S. Army Signal Corps—and an agent of Soviet spymaster Anatoly Yakovlev. Julius recruited other spies, including Ethel's brother, David Greenglass. David, who was part of the top-secret "Manhattan Project" to develop the atomic bomb, stole information from the New Mexico laboratory, which Julius passed on to the Soviets. In 1945 his secret activities were revealed, and five years later the exposure of other members of the spy ring led to the arrest of Julius and Ethel Rosenberg.

The evidence against Ethel was far from substantial: The strongest accusation was made by her sister-in-law, who accused her of typing up the stolen information. Still, both Rosenbergs were sentenced to death in 1951. Two years of appeals followed. International demonstrations and letter-writing campaigns sought mercy, and Ethel, the only woman prisoner in Sing Sing, wrote anguished letters to her husband and two young sons, who were only rarely allowed to visit. In an era when anticommunism was rampant, presidents Harry Truman and Dwight Eisenhower both refused to grant clemency. When Ethel and her husband went to the electric chair in 1953, they were the first American civilians ever executed for espionage.

Betsy Ross presents the flag to George Washington and members of Congress.

independence. Ross, who had sewn flags for Pennsylvania, slightly reworked Washington's rough sketch of the banner, suggesting that the stars have five points instead of six. The "Stars and Stripes" was adopted as the national flag by the Continental Congress on June 14, 1777.

Elizabeth ("Betsy") Ross (1752–1836)
Patriot, seamstress

BETSY GRISCOM, A SKILLED SEAMSTRESS, WAS raised a Quaker in Philadelphia. After her marriage in 1773 to John Ross, an Episcopalian, Betsy was expelled from the Society of Friends. Later she would join the Free Quakers, patriots who rejected Quakerism's traditional pacifist stance and supported the American Revolution.

The Rosses started an upholstery business together. After John was fatally wounded while serving in the militia in 1776, Betsy continued to operate the family business on her own, making it highly profitable. She married twice more and gave birth to seven daughters.

The story that has made Betsy Ross part of American legend—and which historians are still trying to substantiate—is that, in June 1776, George Washington visited her shop and asked her to make a flag for the nation that would soon be declaring its

Policarpa Salavarrieta ("La Pola") (1795–1817)
Patriot

POLICARPA SALAVARRIETA WAS BORN IN A Colombian mountain village at a time when the Colombian people were growing dissatisfied with Spanish rule. Creoles like Policarpa, people of Spanish descent who were born in South America, were deprived of many advantages reserved for native Spaniards. Native South Americans and other people who did not have any Spanish blood were even more disadvantaged.

Policarpa, who was intelligent and independent, became a seamstress. She also absorbed the revolutionary beliefs of her brothers and their teacher, Friar Diego Padilla. In 1810, when she was 15 years old, the Creoles overthrew the royal government and set up their own. However, the Spanish returned six years later and, in what became known as the Reign of Terror, violently reconquered the country. Many revolutionaries were executed without trial.

Policarpa realized that she could use her position as a seamstress, working inside Spanish households, to gather useful information for the revolutionary cause. In addition to passing on overheard intelligence, she gave refuge to guerrilla soldiers as part of an underground network and helped political prisoners escape. At the age of 22, she was captured, imprisoned, and sentenced to death before a firing squad. She remained dignified and defiant to the end, delivering a speech that inspired the Colombian people to continue fighting. Two years later they drove the Spanish out for good, a fitting revenge for the national heroine known as "La Pola."

Deborah Sampson (1760–1827)
Soldier

IN 1782 AN UNUSUALLY CLEAN-SHAVEN MAN NAMED Robert Shurtleff enlisted in the Continental Army to fight against the British in the Revolutionary War. "He" was actually Deborah Sampson. Thanks to her height, strength, and capability, Sampson experienced the independence and adventure usually afforded only to men. However, she also endured the horrors of war and was wounded in battle. While hospitalized with a fever, her identity was discovered. It is an indication of her bravery that she received an honorable discharge from the army.

Sampson, a descendant of the pilgrim Priscilla Alden, was from Plympton, Massachusetts. She had worked as a servant and schoolteacher before joining the army. After returning to women's clothes, she eventually married a farmer, Benjamin Gannett, and had three children. Stories about her adventures began to circulate, and a biography, *The Female Review* (1797), which greatly exaggerated the truth, was published. In 1802 Sampson began appearing onstage in her uniform, delivering lectures to audiences who were as impressed by her brave deeds as they were shocked by her masquerade. Because her war wounds never healed completely, she suffered from poor health but was awarded pensions by the government in recognition of her military service.

Philippa Duke Schuyler (1931–1967)
Musician, writer

PHILIPPA SCHUYLER CRAWLED AT FOUR MONTHS old, walked at eight months, and read by the time she was two. Her father, George Schuyler, was African American, while her mother, Josephine Cogdell, was white. Although they came from different backgrounds, both were journalists. Philippa grew up in the society of artists and intellectuals in New York City. Her parents encouraged her talents, hoping her success would set an example and improve relations between the races. She kept to a strict diet of healthy foods and was mostly schooled at home by her mother.

Schuyler's career began at age three, when she learned to play the piano. By the time she was five, she was performing in public and writing her own musical compositions. Her first orchestral work, composed when she was 13, was performed by the New York Philharmonic. The public was fascinated by her, and articles about her appeared in many magazines. After graduating from high school at age 15, Schuyler traveled the world, performing on the piano, giving lectures, and becoming fluent in several languages. She wrote five books and worked as a news correspondent, braving the dangers of war and revolution. Despite all her achievements, she still faced the barriers of race and gender prejudice, and her letters reveal a troubled young woman struggling to find her true place in the world. She died when her helicopter crashed as she was trying to rescue schoolchildren from a battle zone during the Vietnam War.

Mary Jane Seacole (1805–1881)
War relief worker, entrepreneur

MARY GRANT WAS BORN IN KINGSTON, JAMAICA, the daughter of a Scottish military officer and a Jamaican healer and hotelkeeper. Her marriage at age 31 to Edward Seacole was brief; he died within the year. After that Mary took over her mother's hotel and worked as a healer, developing her own remedies from local plants and constantly teaching herself new medical skills. During epidemics of cholera, dysentery, and yellow fever, Mary was there, tirelessly nursing. She also established hotels throughout the Caribbean.

When the Crimean War broke out in 1853, Seacole traveled to England and offered her services as a nurse a few months later. She was rejected, most likely because of the color of her skin. Undaunted, she traveled to the Crimean Peninsula using her own resources. She built the British Hotel near Balaklava, making it a comfortable place where wounded soldiers could recuperate, and served as a volunteer

> "[A]s often as the bad news came, I thought it my duty to ride up to the hut of the sufferer and do my woman's work. But I felt it deeply. How could it be otherwise? . . . Mind you, a day was a long time to give to sorrow in the Crimea. . . . Others have described the horrors of those fatal trenches; but their real history has never been written, and perhaps it is as well that so harrowing a tale should be left in oblivion."
>
> MARY SEACOLE
> *The Wonderful Adventures of Mrs. Seacole in Many Lands*

nurse alongside Florence Nightingale. Seacole's heroism in tending wounded soldiers on the battlefield, even under gunfire, was glowingly reported in the British newspapers. After the war ended in 1856, contributions were raised to save her from bankruptcy. Her autobiography, *The Wonderful Adventures of Mrs. Seacole in Many Lands* (1857), became a best-seller.

Hannah Senesh (1921–1944)
Resistance fighter, poet

HANNAH SENESH GREW UP IN BUDAPEST, Hungary, proud of her Jewish heritage and aware of anti-Semitism from an early age. She was a talented writer and dreamed of a university education. In 1938, when Hungary announced that it would side with Germany in World War II, she immigrated to Palestine and, after studying agriculture, lived on a kibbutz (communal farm).

Although she was happy farming and writing poetry in the Jewish homeland, Senesh was troubled by the suffering of European Jews. In 1943 she joined the Haganah, an underground Jewish army working with the Allies. After training with the British army, Senesh's commando unit was at last allowed to go to the rescue of other Jews still in occupied territories. She parachuted into Yugoslavia and led her small group through enemy gunfire to Hungary despite warnings of danger. She was captured by Hungarian police and turned over to the Nazis, who attempted to gain information about the Allied radio code by torturing her. Even when her mother was also threatened with torture, Senesh refused to speak. With American and Russian troops closing in, she was executed by a firing squad, but her words of inspiration live on in her published poetry and diary.

Caterina Sforza (1462–1509)
Warrior, ruler

BEAUTIFUL, BOLD CATERINA SFORZA RULED THE Italian provinces of Forlì and Imola, valiantly defending her lands from the armies of surrounding regions, popes, and the French. Although her first husband was ruler in name, she wielded the real

power. She controlled her troops with iron discipline and delivered cruel punishments to her enemies. Once she rode into battle when seven months pregnant. During a later conflict, her children were taken hostage, but she refused to surrender her castle, proclaiming that she could always have more babies. Pope Alexander VI condemned Caterina's immoral behavior with her several lovers. However, truth be known, he was not much better behaved; he hoped to acquire her lands by discrediting her.

The illegitimate daughter of Galeazza Sforza, who became Duke of Milan, Caterina had received an excellent education and had been allowed to indulge in hunting and other athletic activities. At age 15 she married Girolamo Riario. He was murdered in 1488, and Caterina took brutal revenge on his killers. She continued to rule in her oldest son's name and soon married Giovanni de' Medici. In 1500 she was finally defeated by Cesare Borgia, who subjected her to abuse for a year. After her release she devoted herself to training one of her children, Giovanni dalle Bande Nere, to become the greatest military leader of the Medici family.

Kate Shelley (1865–1912)
Heroine

During a terrible rainstorm on the night of July 6, 1881, 15-year-old Kate Shelley and her mother were huddled inside their cottage next to a railroad track in rural Iowa. They watched as an inspection train began to cross nearby Honey Creek. Weakened by the pounding rain and wind, the bridge over the creek collapsed. Realizing that an express train was due within the hour, Kate set out on foot for the Moingona station, more than a mile away. She had to cross the Des Moines River on one of the highest and longest wooden trestle bridges in the country, a dangerous journey even in daylight and good weather. Kate crawled on her hands and knees, ripping her skin and clothes, her lamp extinguished by the storm. She made it to the station just in time to warn the stationmaster to stop the express and then led a crew to rescue the survivors from the inspection train.

The "Heroine of Honey Creek" became a celebrity, receiving awards and a college scholarship. A newspaper campaign raised enough money to pay off her family's mortgage. Shelley was eventually appointed the Moingona station agent and given other honors by the railroad company, including having the train make a special stop at her front door whenever she needed to ride it.

Karen Silkwood (1946–1974)
Nuclear worker, activist

On the night of November 13, 1974, Karen Silkwood left Crescent, Oklahoma, on her way to meet a *New York Times* reporter in Oklahoma City. She planned to give him information concerning health and safety violations committed by her employer, the Kerr-McGee nuclear power plant. Ten minutes into the drive, Silkwood's car plunged off the road and crashed. Authorities ruled her death an accident, but a manila folder filled with incriminating documentation, known to have been in her possession, wasn't found at the scene. Evidence later showed that her car had been rammed from behind.

Silkwood, a Texas native and divorced mother of three children, had been a technician for Kerr-McKee for two years. She was active in the workers' union and had agreed to carry out an investigation at the plant after attending a meeting with the Atomic Energy Commission in Washington, D.C. She knew that plant workers weren't warned of the dangers of the highly toxic plutonium created in the nuclear fission process. In addition to discovering

Karen Silkwood with her children

radioactive residue in the company cafeteria, Silkwood found that she herself had somehow been contaminated by radioactivity. Investigations following her death revealed that the plant was indeed guilty of violations and that plutonium had been planted in her apartment. The mystery surrounding Silkwood's death—still unsolved—drew attention to the questionable safety practices of the nuclear power industry.

Wallis Warfield Simpson (Duchess of Windsor) (1896–1986)
Socialite

WALLIS WARFIELD GREW UP IN THE HIGHER circles of Baltimore society and was known for her liveliness and elegant sense of style. After her debut she married a navy pilot, mingled with diplomats, and gained a reputation for scandalous behavior. In 1928, having divorced the pilot a few months earlier, she married a British shipping tycoon named Ernest Simpson and moved with him to London. There she became part of fashionable British society. One day in 1930, at a luncheon, she was seated next to the man who would change the course of her life: Edward, the prince of Wales and future king of England.

The prince, captivated by her independent spirit, began to appear publicly with Mrs. Simpson. After he was crowned King Edward VIII in January 1936, their romantic relationship could no longer be ignored— the now twice-divorced American was an unthinkable candidate for queen. On December 10, Edward renounced the throne in order to marry the woman he loved. His title became Edward, Duke of Windsor.

The Duke and Duchess of Windsor

The royal family neither attended Edward and Wallis's 1937 wedding nor spoke to them afterward. However, the couple remained popular members of the jet set (the wealthy, international crowd often seen at fashionable resorts). He later served as governor of the Bahamas, while she worked for the Red Cross. After World War II, they settled outside Paris, still very much in love.

Samantha Smith (1972–1985)
Goodwill ambassador

SAMANTHA SMITH WAS AN ORDINARY TEN-YEAR-OLD living in Manchester, Maine, when she decided to write a letter to the leader of the Soviet Union, Yuri Andropov. Worried about the possibility of nuclear war between his country and hers, she candidly expressed her thoughts on the importance of peace. To her surprise Andropov wrote back, assuring Samantha that his country wanted peace, too. He also invited her to visit the Soviet Union, which she did in July 1983, accompanied by her family. The world's media paid close attention to the young ambassador, who proved to be a charming and effective advocate for peace.

From then on Samantha found herself doing her homework assignments between traveling and speaking engagements. She also wrote a book and was cast in a prime-time television series after her acting talent became apparent during her public appearances. In 1985 she and her father were returning from a filming session in London when their plane crashed. People around the world, from peasants to presidents, mourned the death of such a promising symbol of hope. Samantha's mother started a foundation in her honor to continue her mission of peace education.

Hannah Snell (1723–1792)
Soldier

ENGLISH-BORN HANNAH SNELL HAD BEEN MARRIED to a Dutch sailor named James Summs for less than a year when he abandoned her in 1745. Determined to find him, she took her brother-in-law's

name, James Gray, disguised herself as a man, and joined a British troop of foot soldiers. She participated in a march against the Scottish troops of Bonnie Prince Charlie, who sought (unsuccessfully) to seize the British throne. She then took service as a cook and steward onboard a navy ship bound for India. When the English attacked the French at Pondicherry on the Madras coast, she reportedly received wounds, which she tended in secret to avoid discovery.

On her way back to England in 1750, Hannah learned that Summs had been executed. Once home, she not only revealed her true identity but published her best-selling memoirs, *The Female Soldier* (1750). She also made stage appearances in uniform, telling her story with sensational elaboration. Snell was granted a pension in recognition of her service, set up an inn called The Female Warrior outside London, and married two more times. During her final years, she suffered from mental illness. She died in Bethlehem Hospital, an insane asylum popularly known as Bedlam.

Valerie Solanas (1937?–1988)
Militant feminist, attempted murderer

DURING THE 1960s VALERIE SOLANAS WAS PART of the counterculture scene in New York City. Although she had a degree in psychology from the University of Maryland, she made her living panhandling and writing about her experiences on the street. She was the founder and only member of the Society for Cutting Up Men (SCUM); her self-published *SCUM Manifesto* (1968) proclaimed her violent brand of feminism. Solanas became obsessed with artist, filmmaker, and popular-culture guru Andy Warhol. When he refused to produce a film script she'd written, she began calling him and sending him letters that revealed an unbalanced mind. To placate her Warhol gave her money and cast her in a small part in one of his films.

Solanas was also obsessed with publisher Maurice Girodias, and on June 3, 1968, she set out to kill him. Girodias wasn't at home, so she went to Warhol's studio instead and shot the artist in the chest. Warhol survived after extensive surgery. Although most feminists reject Solanas's extreme methods, she did receive some sympathy. She turned herself in to the police and was examined at psychiatric hospitals until she was declared fit to stand trial. She pled guilty, served three years in jail, then led a quiet life. Her death in San Francisco was caused by pneumonia.

Belle Starr (1848–1889)
Outlaw

MYRA BELL SHIRLEY WAS BORN IN MISSOURI, BUT her family moved to Texas after her brother was killed by Union troops in 1863. The brother may have belonged to the Quantrill Raiders, a Civil War guerrilla troop that later split into smaller gangs, the most notorious of which were led by the Younger brothers and Frank and Jesse James. Later most of these outlaws became associates of Belle's. Her first child, Pearl, was probably fathered by Cole Younger, who hid at her house for a time. Belle next joined up with bank robber Jim Reed, with whom she had a son, Edward. She and Reed lived briefly in California and then returned to Texas, where Belle styled herself the "Bandit Queen" and rode her racehorse, Venus, at breakneck speed through the streets. Soon after carrying out a dramatic stagecoach holdup near Austin, Reed was killed in a gunfight.

Belle moved to the Oklahoma Territory, where in 1880 she married a Cherokee Indian named Sam Starr. Their ranch became a hideout for outlaws, and Belle gained a reputation for masterminding livestock raids. In 1883 the Starrs were convicted of horse stealing and served several months at the federal penitentiary in Detroit, Michigan. Belle was connected romantically with other outlaws, all of whom met unsavory ends, and she herself was killed by a shot in the back. The murderer was never identified.

> "Arrest her! Oh, you try that game?
> In Dallas many years ago
> The county sheriff tried the same.
> One rapid shot, the rest you know;
> Still Belle loves to give her name:
> Please let me have your best cigar,
> I'm Belle Starr."
>
> from "Belle Star,"
> a poem of the Old West,
> author unknown

A Controversial Saint

Although no one denies the good works that Edith Stein performed, many Jewish people question whether Pope John Paul II should have made her a saint. They feel that, by claiming Stein as a martyr for the Catholic faith, the Pope has obscured the fact that she was killed for being Jewish, not because she was a nun. The Vatican, on the other hand, argues that it is honoring her as a Jew and a remarkable Christian, as well as paying homage to the nuns and priests who died at Auschwitz.

Edith Stein (1891–1942)
Nun

BORN INTO AN ORTHODOX JEWISH FAMILY IN Breslau, Germany (now Wroclaw, Poland), Edith Stein attended the University of Göttingen, where she became the protégée of Edmund Husserl, founder of phenomenology. When Husserl moved to the University of Freiburg, Edith went with him as his assistant. She became a respected author and philosopher, interested in feminist issues and religious thought.

In 1922 Edith converted to Roman Catholicism, having been profoundly affected by the autobiography of St. Teresa of Ávila. She began teaching at a Dominican girls' school in Speyer, where she lived devoutly and austerely. She served briefly as a lecturer at the Institute for Pedagogy at Münster in 1932 but lost the position when the newly elected Nazi government banned Jews from academic posts. Entering the Carmelite convent at Cologne as a nun, she took the name Teresa Benedicta of the Cross.

In 1938 the increasingly violent persecution of Jews in Germany forced Edith to move to a Dutch convent. The Nazis invaded Holland four years later and arrested all Jewish-born converted Catholics. Edith was sent to the Auschwitz concentration camp, where she gave comfort to other prisoners before she died in the gas chamber. In recognition of her martyrdom, Pope John Paul II recognized her as a saint in 1998.

Kerri Strug (1977–)

Gymnast

T OWARD THE END OF THE WOMEN'S GROUP gymnastics competition at the 1996 Summer Olympics in Atlanta, Georgia, the American women's team held a slim advantage. The pressure was on the last American contestant, Kerri Strug, to clench the gold medal for the team by getting a high score in the vault event.

Strug's first vault was less than perfect, and as she landed, she heard something snap in her leg. Nevertheless, she decided to try again (gymnasts are allowed two vaults, and the better score is used for the team score). This time she received a high score but collapsed in agony. Her coach, Bela Karolyi, carried her in his arms to receive the gold medal with her team. She had badly sprained her ankle and had to withdraw from the upcoming individual competition. Later Strug found out that her first score would have won the gold, but fans celebrated her as a heroine for her sacrifice.

Strug had begun taking gymnastics at age three, partly because her older sister and brother were gymnasts, too. A self-motivated perfectionist, she left her family in Arizona to train at Karolyi's gym in Houston when she was 13. Strug's career was impressive; she was the youngest athlete at the 1992 Olympics. Even so, until 1996 she was considered a shy "understudy" to more celebrated teammates. After the Olympics she decided to continue her education and enrolled at the University of California at Los Angeles.

Mary Eugenia Surratt (1820–1865)

Accused conspirator

A T THE OUTBREAK OF THE CIVIL WAR, MARY Surratt found herself widowed and destitute. She moved to Washington, D.C., and opened a boardinghouse there. Her son John also lived in the city. Mary may have been unaware that he not only worked as a spy for the Confederacy but also was involved in a plot to kidnap President Abraham Lincoln. He and his fellow conspirators, led by John Wilkes Booth, a well-known actor, met at Mary's rooming house.

When it became clear that the South had lost the war, Booth decided to assassinate Lincoln rather than abduct him. He carried out the plan on April 14, 1865, shooting the president during a performance at Ford's Theater. Booth himself died 12 days later trying to escape. Mary Surratt was arrested along with several others, although her son eluded capture. Emotions were running high after the war; the conspirators were not given an impartial hearing by the military commission. The evidence against Mary was especially vague and was provided by a notoriously unreliable witness. Most historians believe she was innocent of anything other than owning the boardinghouse where the conspirators met. Nevertheless, she was the first woman hanged by the United States government.

Elizabeth Tashjian (1910s?–)

Curator of nut museum, performance artist

E LIZABETH TASHJIAN'S CHILDHOOD INTEREST IN nuts grew into an obsession that led her to turn her Victorian mansion in Old Lyme, Connecticut, into the "Nut Museum" in 1972. The museum's extensive collection includes works of art depicting or made from nuts, which she began creating while attending New York City's National Academy School of Fine Arts in the 1930s. It also houses a selection of antique nutcrackers, a sculpture garden decorated in a nut and nutcracker motif, and, of course, nuts of every type, from ordinary to rare, including the world's largest nut, a 35-pound (16-kg) coco-de-mer.

Tashjian personally shows visitors around the museum after charging an admission fee that includes one nut. In addition to delivering lectures on nut history to museum guests, she has made several television appearances, singing songs about nuts and explaining her theory that humans are descended from nuts, as well as other original ideas. When part of the museum's collection was eaten by squirrels, Tashjian quipped that they might be "starting a nut museum of their own."

Corrie ten Boom (1892–1983)
Missionary

CORRIE TEN BOOM SPENT THE FIRST 48 YEARS OF her life learning the clock-making trade and working beside her father, Casper, in his shop in the Dutch city of Haarlem. Casper endowed his children with a strong Christian faith. As he grew older, Corrie and her sister Betsie took care of him. In 1940 the Germans invaded Holland and the ten Booms' Jewish neighbors began to disappear.

> While imprisoned, Corrie ten Boom found great solace in packages from the Red Cross, because they were evidence that friendly people were thinking of the captives. At the same time, the delicacies only made her more aware of her isolation. She describes examining the contents of a box : ". . . [B]iscuits, a croquette, licorice. But why is there not happiness in my heart? Alone. . . . I think that later (will there be a later?) I won't ever like to eat candies alone by myself. Somebody will have to share and then I will think of cell 384."
>
> CORRIE TEN BOOM
> *Prison Letters*, 1975

Although both Corrie and Betsie suffered from ill health, they devoted endless energy to organizing an underground movement to help Jews escape and often hid refugees in their own home. In February 1944 the sisters and their father were arrested. Casper died soon after, but Corrie and Betsie were eventually sent to the Ravensbruck concentration camp in Germany. There, while suffering from deprivation and hard labor, they still helped fellow prisoners endure in the face of hardship. Corrie was released soon after Betsie's death in December 1944.

Returning to Holland, Corrie continued to help those in danger from the Nazis until the country was liberated in May 1945. She then turned to the needs of war victims and opened rehabilitation centers. She also began traveling, telling her story of survival around the world as a Christian missionary. She wrote many books, including the autobiographical best-seller *The Hiding Place* (1971).

Billy Tipton (1914–1989)
Jazz musician

BILLY TIPTON WAS A TALENTED JAZZ MUSICIAN who played saxophone and piano with the Billy Tipton Trio and other groups in small-town clubs throughout America. Fans often wondered

why he didn't take advantage of the opportunities he had to hit the big time. What they didn't realize was that Billy had reason to avoid the limelight: He had been born Dorothy Lucille.

Dorothy came of age in the 1930s, when jazz was reaching the heights of popularity, especially in her hometown of Kansas City. She quickly realized that, as a woman, she would never be able to establish herself as a musician, so she began wearing men's clothes, obtained new legal documents, and became—for all practical purposes—a man.

Although it must have been difficult to maintain, the new role gave Billy the freedom he needed. Friends were impressed by his gentleness, love for animals and children, and fine sense of humor. He and his last wife, Kitty Oakes, adopted and raised three boys. In his mature years, while working as a theatrical agent in Spokane, Washington, Tipton fell ill but, as usual, refused to see a doctor. Only after Billy's death was the secret revealed, to the surprise of those who had known him, including bandmates and five former wives.

Tituba (late 17th century)
Accused witch, slave

IN THE WINTER OF 1691, A SMALL GROUP OF women and girls began gathering at the home of the Reverend Samuel Parris in the Puritan settlement of Salem, Massachusetts. They came to listen to the stories told by Parris's slave, Tituba, who had been brought with her husband from the West Indies. Tituba's tales of life on her island home abounded with accounts of rituals such as fortune-telling, spirit-talking, and herbal healing. The stories had a strange effect on two of her young listeners, who began to behave oddly. Questioned by local ministers, the girls claimed that they had been bewitched by Tituba and two old beggar women. Thus began the infamous Salem witch trials. From March to October of 1692, a total of 150 suspects were imprisoned, and 19 were hanged.

During her trial Tituba was forced to confess guilt and to accuse others of witchcraft. Hysteria raged throughout the colony as more and more people were unjustly accused, sometimes out of malice. When upstanding citizens, including wives of ministers and the colony's governor, were named

as witches, the civil magistrates began to question the integrity of their "investigations." Gradually the people regained their senses, and the trials were brought to a close. It is believed that Parris sold Tituba while she was in jail and that she was eventually released to her new owner. The rest of her story is unknown.

La Toffania (1653–1723)
Poisoner

AT THE END OF THE 17TH CENTURY, WOMEN IN Naples, Italy, who wanted a handy way out of an oppressive marriage knew just what to do. They visited Toffania to purchase a bottle of her "Manna of St. Nicholas of Bari," supposedly a miraculous medicine or beauty ointment. It was actually a lethal poison, containing liberal amounts of arsenic. A large dose killed swiftly; a series of smaller doses simulated a progressive illness—and drew out the agony of death. "Acqua toffania," as it came to be known, attracted buyers from many parts of Europe.

In 1719 authorities noticed that large numbers of Neapolitan married men were dying. Their investigations led to Toffania, who fled to a convent. By custom she should have been safe in that religious sanctuary, but after rumors surfaced that she had poisoned the city's drinking water, she was dragged out by soldiers. She confessed under torture to the murder, directly or indirectly, of more than 600 people and was executed in 1723.

Trung Trac (?–43)

Trung Nhi, (?–43)
Warriors, revolutionaries

IN 111 B.C.E. VIETNAM WAS CONQUERED BY THE Han Dynasty of China. The Chinese sought to impose their values, including female subservience, upon the Vietnamese, whose women were traditionally respected and had more freedom. Around 39 C.E. the Vietnamese people began to grow restless. To intimidate them, a Chinese overlord assassinated Thi Sach, Lord of Chau Dien. Thi Sach's widow, Trung

Trac, responded by organizing a rebellion with the help of her younger sister, Trung Nhi. They exhibited strong leadership, calling together the tribal lords and forming an army of 80,000. Many of the soldiers were women, and the sisters' mother was one of 36 female generals. The rebels marched on the Chinese commander's headquarters, forcing him to flee. Although the sisters' forces were relatively untrained, within a year they had beaten the seasoned Chinese troops into retreat and won territory from Hue into southern China.

The sisters proclaimed themselves queens of an independent state, but after three years the Chinese general Ma Yüan defeated their army near present-day Hanoi, crushing them as they retreated. The sisters committed suicide by drowning themselves where the Day and Red rivers meet. The Han Dynasty then maintained its control in Vietnam until 221 C.E. Although the Trung sisters' rebellion was brief, it planted the seeds for future independence. They are honored every year with a national holiday that usually falls in March.

Elizabeth Van Lew (1818–1900)
Unionist, spy

ELIZABETH VAN LEW WAS DESPISED IN HER hometown of Richmond, Virginia, for openly declaring herself an abolitionist during the Civil War, but she won the admiration of the Union soldiers she helped to escape from prison and sometimes hid in her home.

Born into a wealthy family, Van Lew was educated in Philadelphia. Her antislavery views were formed early, and she convinced her family to free their slaves in the 1850s. Throughout the war, she visited Union prisoners in the Richmond jail, bringing food and other supplies and carrying out useful military information for the North. During the year-long Siege of Richmond from 1864 to 1865, she organized her family's former slaves to help gather and pass information. Her activities aroused suspicions, so she pretended to be mentally unbalanced, earning the nickname "Crazy Bet."

When Richmond fell in April 1865, Van Lew raised a Union flag and received the protection of General Ulysses Grant. Her neighbors, outraged by her betrayal, boycotted the family's hardware

business. She became a social outcast and was reduced to poverty until Grant and other grateful Northern officers provided her with a modest income. She spent her final years in Richmond, living in the family mansion where she had hidden so many Union soldiers.

La Voisin (?–1680)
Witch, poisoner

CATHERINE DESHAYES MONVOISIN—BETTER known as La Voisin—may not have had magical powers, but the Frenchwoman was a shrewd reader of human nature. After her husband's business failed, she turned her talents for "fortune-telling" into a thriving enterprise, attracting wealthy clients to her cottage on the outskirts of Paris. King Louis XIV's powerful mistress, Madame de Montespan, was one of her many famous customers. Some people came to her to ask for love potions and "magic" charms, while others demanded more certain ways of getting what they wanted. La Voisin would eventually be accused of selling poisons that were used to murder thousands of people. She also presided at "black masses," which supposedly involved the sacrifice of infants, for those wishing to invoke unholy powers to achieve their ambitions.

Others set up shop to sell magic potions, calling themselves "alchemists" to hide the real nature of their business, but La Voisin was by far the most successful. She became immensely rich. The authorities suspected her, but they couldn't prove anything until she became involved in a plot to poison the king. She and her accomplices were arrested and tried in a special court. Many aristocrats found themselves banished due to their involvement with La Voisin, and several dozen less fortunate people were condemned to death. La Voisin herself, after three days of torture, was burned to death in a public square.

Ellen Watson (1861–1889)
Accused cattle thief, lynching victim

FOR A CENTURY ELLEN, OR ELLA, WATSON WAS known in Wyoming as "Cattle Kate," a livestock thief and prostitute whose customers often paid for her services with maverick (unbranded)

calves. More recently, however, historians have uncovered a different story.

During the late 19th century in the West, a rivalry arose between the big-business "cattle barons" and settlers from the East. For years the cattle barons had raised their huge herds on the open range—but that land was being broken up by the government into homesteading properties.

Canadian-born Watson was raised in Kansas. After leaving an abusive husband, she led a respectable life as a servant and moved to the Sweetwater River Valley in the late 1880s. She soon attracted the attention of Jim Averill, a local homesteader engaged in an ongoing battle with the cattle barons. The two apparently married but kept it secret so that Ellen could establish her own claim to a homesteading property.

In July 1889 a vigilante group of cattlemen abducted Watson and Averill. It is uncertain whether the men had meant to hang the couple from the beginning or if matters got out of hand, but both Watson and Averill ended up dead. In all their accounts of the event, the local newspapers (which were owned by the cattle barons) described the murder victims as experienced and unprincipled cattle thieves.

Sarah Winchester (1839–1922)
Heiress, eccentric

SARAH WINCHESTER INHERITED $20 MILLION upon the 1880 death of her husband, George, heir to the Winchester rifle fortune. The superstitious widow was moved by a medium's warning that her husband's death, and that of her young daughter several years earlier, had been caused by the spirits of people killed by Winchester rifles. The medium also warned that Sarah herself was in danger unless she was in the process of building a house. Sarah immediately moved from Hartford, Connecticut, to San Jose, California, where she began a 40-year-long construction project.

The house, which is now called the Winchester Mystery House and is open to the public, consists of 160 rooms, although hundreds more were built and torn down while Winchester lived there. It includes secret passageways, trapdoors, walled-off rooms, decorative elements installed upside-down, and stairs leading into thin air—all designed to confuse ghosts. Although she was untrained as an architect, Winchester planned everything herself, met with the foreman daily, and chose the building materials, most of them expensive. She also designed several state-of-the-art features, such as a system for collecting rainwater and recycling the water that had been used on house plants. She kept workers on the job 24 hours a day. Winchester remained veiled, even at home, and turned away all visitors in her efforts to avoid the attention of ghosts, but she did eventually pass to the other side.

Elizabeth ("Betty") Zane (1766?–1831?)
Frontier heroine

FEW DETAILS OF BETTY ZANE'S LIFE CAN BE confirmed, but she is credited with carrying out a daring exploit in the final years of the Revolutionary War. She grew up in Wheeling, West Virginia, a town founded by her older brother,

Ebenezer, and she may have attended school in Philadelphia. According to legend, in September 1782 she had just returned home when Wheeling was attacked by Indians fighting for the British.

The townspeople rushed from their houses to the safety of Fort Henry, only to discover that they hadn't brought enough gunpowder to defend themselves. A volunteer was needed to run to Ebenezer's house, about 40 yards (37 m) away, and bring more powder. Betty stepped forward, declaring that she could more easily be spared than a man. As she raced toward the house, the attackers stopped firing, either astounded at her courage or unwilling to shoot a woman. On her way back, though, they realized what was happening and opened fire. Betty arrived safely at the fort, her clothes pierced with bullet holes, and the townspeople were able to hold out until help arrived.

Betty married twice and spent her final years in Martins Ferry, Ohio. Her story inspired the novel *Betty Zane* (1903) by Zane Grey, her descendant and a prolific Western author.

Betty Zane delivers the gunpowder.

TIME LINE

9th century B.C.E.	Jezebel, the widow of King Ahab of Israel, is assassinated by political rivals who oppose her tyrannical behavior and fanatical devotion to foreign gods.
6th century B.C.E.	The first books that will later make up the Old Testament are recorded.
5th century B.C.E.	Esther, the Jewish wife of the Persian King Ahasuerus, believed to be Xerxes I, saves the Jews from a massacre planned by Haman, a high government official. Esther's heroic deed is still celebrated at the festival of Purim.
2 B.C.E.	Enraged after learning that all of Rome is gossiping about the scandalous behavior of his daughter, Julia, Emperor Augustus banishes her to a remote island.
1st century	The books that will later make up the New Testament are written down. They will tell of the religious teachings of Jesus, born in the early years of the century to a woman named Mary.
39–43	The Vietnamese sisters Trung Trac and Trung Nhi lead a revolution. After overthrowing their Chinese rulers, they preside together over an independent Vietnam for about three years, until the Chinese reconquer the country.
5th century	When her father is unable to fulfill his duties with the Chinese army, Hua Mu-Lan takes his place and for many years manages to conceal her true identity, while proving her bravery

in battle. Centuries later she will be celebrated in plays and poetry as the most famous Chinese woman warrior.

632	Prophet Muhammad, founder of the Islamic religion, dies. His young wife, Aishah, continues to spread his ideas.
1040s	According to legend Anglo-Saxon noblewoman Lady Godiva rides naked through the marketplace of Coventry, risking her modesty in order to save the citizens of the town from the heavy taxes imposed by her husband, Leofric.

Héloïse

1118	Héloïse, young, educated, and from an upper-class background, falls in love with her tutor, Peter Abelard. They secretly marry and have a child.
1338	Scottish folk heroine Lady Agnes Dunbar ("Black Agnes") defends her castle during a five-month siege by the English.
1492	Explorer Christopher Columbus lands on an island in the Bahamas,

most probably San Salvador, and claims this New World in the name of the Spanish King Ferdinand.

1503   Lucrezia Borgia's father, Rodrigo, is accidentally poisoned by her brother, Cesare. Lucrezia had often been used by her unscrupulous male family members—or acted as an accomplice in their political intrigues (history provides conflicting accounts). After her father's death, however, she appears to have led an exemplary life.

1519   The Spanish, led by Hernán Cortés, arrive in Mexico. Malintzin, a slave, is given by her owners to Cortés as a gift. She becomes his translator, adviser, and mistress.

1553   On July 10 Lady Jane Grey is declared queen of England by a group of Protestants hoping to control the country. Nine days later the true heir to the throne, the Catholic Mary Tudor, claims her title. Lady Jane, an unwilling pawn in this game, will eventually be executed for treason.

1547   Henry II becomes king of France. He is married to Catherine de Médicis, but he is dominated by his beautiful, older mistress, Diane de Poitiers.

1598   Italian nobleman Francesco Cenci is murdered by an unknown assassin. It is soon revealed that the person who

hired the killer is Francesco's young and beautiful daughter, Beatrice.

1607   According to popular lore, Captain John Smith, the leader of the British colonists in Jamestown, Virginia, is captured by Algonquin Indians. His life is saved by the Native American princess Pocahontas.

1669   Actress Nell Gwyn, who has recently become the mistress of King Charles II of England, appears onstage for the last time. After the closing of the play—John Dryden's *Conquest of Granada by the Spaniards*—she will devote herself exclusively to the king.

1692   The Salem Witch Trials. Puritan reverend Samuel Parris leads the town of Salem, Massachusetts, in a hysterical "witch hunt." Fourteen women and five men are hanged, one man is pressed to death, and many more people, including Parris's slave from the West Indies, Tituba, are imprisoned.

1720   Pirates Anne Bonny and Mary Read, notorious for their activities in the Caribbean, are captured by the British government.

1775–1783   The American Revolution. The Declaration of Independence is signed in July 1776. Toward the end of the war, Deborah Sampson enlists in the army as Robert Shurtleff. She acquits herself so bravely that when her true sex is revealed, she is granted an honorable discharge.

1788   The first English settlement (Port Jackson) is established in Australia in the eastern territory known as New South Wales. The British use their new land as a penal colony. Criminal Margaret Catchpole arrives in 1801, after stealing a horse.

Beatrice Cenci

1789–1799   Revolution in France. In 1793 French patriot Charlotte Corday walks from Normandy to Paris to assassinate the radical revolutionary Jean-Paul Marat.

1790   Flora MacDonald dies in Scotland. A heroine ever since she helped Bonnie Prince Charlie escape from the British 45 years earlier, she is buried in a sheet once slept on by the prince.

1810   Mexican patriot Gertrudis Bocanegra convinces her husband to quit the Spanish army and join a Mexican rebel group. She will be executed for her role in the rebel movement and its fight for independence in 1817.

1819   Soldier Simón Bolívar leads a rebellion against the Spanish that results in the liberation of much of South America. Colombian rebel Policarpa Salavarrieta also played an important role in inspiring the people to fight the Spanish, but she was executed in 1817, too early to share the victory.

1831   Helena Hahn is born in the Ukraine. By 1875 she will be world-famous as Madame Blavatsky, mystic and founder of the Theosophical Society.

Helena Blavatsky

1848   The first women's rights convention is held in Seneca Falls, New York.

Gold is discovered in California. Approximately 80,000 prospectors arrive there by 1849, and even more come after the transcontinental railroad is built in 1869. "Calamity Jane" Cannary and outlaws Belle Starr, Pearl Hart, and Poker Alice Ivers are among the women who make their living—legally or otherwise—in the "Wild West."

1853–1856   The Crimean War. Turkey declares war on Russia and is joined by Britain and France the following year. Although Britain rejects her offers to help, Jamaican nurse Mary Seacole joins the war effort, tending to injured British troops.

1861–1865   The Civil War in America. Belle Boyd and Rose Greenhow serve the Confederate army as spies, while the abolitionist Southerner Elizabeth Van Lew serves as a spy for the Union army. Canadian Sarah Edmonds disguises herself as a man and enlists in the Union army.

1862   The Homestead Act offers 160 acres (65 ha) of land in the Midwest and West for a small fee to anyone who wants to go. In 1889 Ellen Watson and Jim Averill will be killed for trying to establish homesteads on land occupied by powerful cattle barons in Wyoming.

1865   On April 14, President Abraham Lincoln is killed by John Wilkes Booth, an actor and supporter of the recently defeated Confederacy. Among the people executed for being part of the assassination conspiracy is boardinghouse keeper Mary Surratt.

1871   The Great Chicago Fire is believed to have started after Mrs. Patrick

O'Leary's cow kicks over a kerosene lantern—even after it is officially established that Mrs. O'Leary was asleep in bed when the fire started.

1876   Marian Anthon marries wealthy Stuyvesant Fish. "Mamie's" lavish, eccentric parties will bring life to the New York social scene, long ruled by the established upper classes.

Marian Fish

1892   Lizzie Borden is the top suspect in the brutal murder of her parents. Although she is not convicted of the crime, a rhyme about her is passed down for generations: "Lizzie Borden took and ax / and gave her mother 40 whacks. / And when she saw what she had done / she gave her father 41."

1905   Dutch-born Margaretha Zelle finally achieves stardom as an exotic dancer under the stage name Mata Hari. Within a few years she will be recruited as a spy for the Germans.

1912   On her maiden voyage, the huge passenger ship S.S. *Titanic* hits an iceberg in the Northern Atlantic Ocean and sinks in less than three hours. One of the survivors, Denver millionaire Molly Brown, helps to organize women and children into lifeboats. She is hailed as a hero.

1914–1918   World War I. In 1915 German authorities arrest British Red Cross Nurse Edith Cavell for helping Allied military prisoners to escape. She is tried, convicted, and executed by a firing squad.

1917   The Russian Revolution. The former leader, Czar Nicholas II, is assassinated the next year along with his family. Rumors circulate that there may be survivors, and in 1920 Anna Anderson claims to be the princess Anastasia.

1918   All British women over 30 years old are given the right to vote, five years too late to save militant suffragist Emily Davison. On Derby Day in 1913, she staged a one-woman protest, running out onto the track after the race had started. She was struck and killed by a horse that belonged to the king.

1920   Prohibition begins. The 18th Amendment to the U.S. Constitution bans the manufacture, sale, and transportation of alcohol. Gangsters set up illegal saloons, or speakeasies. Violent gang rivalries develop. Prohibition will end in 1933 with the passage of the 21st Amendment.

The 19th Amendment to the U.S. Constitution grants women's suffrage. It goes into effect on August 26th.

1929   The Great Depression begins after the stock market crash in late October. Unemployment rates skyrocket, and Americans endure poverty and hunger. Some, such as Bonnie Parker and her partner, Clyde Barrow, turn to a life of crime.

1936–1939   The Spanish Civil War erupts between nationalist rebels and the weak republican government. Among the American expatriate writers, artists, and intellectuals drawn to the cause is Tina Modotti, a photographer and Communist spy.

1939–1945 World War II. Adolf Hitler's mistress, Eva Braun, leads a comfortable life away from the action. Others, such as Jewish heroines Haviva Reik and Hannah Senesh, lose their lives trying to save as many people as possible.

1951 A federal judge finds Julius and Ethel Rosenberg guilty of selling atomic secrets to the Soviet Union. They are sentenced to death and executed two years later, despite the efforts of many who protest their conviction.

1955 Murderer Ruth Ellis is the last woman hanged in Great Britain.

1963 On November 22, President John Kennedy is shot while riding with his wife, Jacqueline, in a motorcade through Dallas, Texas.

1964–1975 The Vietnam War. Former child prodigy and composer Philippa Duke Schuyler dies in a helicopter crash in 1967, while trying to rescue children from the war-torn region.

1974 Patricia Hearst, heiress to her grandfather William Randolph Hearst's newspaper fortune, is abducted from her home in San Francisco by a militant group that calls itself the Symbionese Liberation Army.

1986 The U.S. space shuttle *Challenger* explodes just over a minute after liftoff. One of the seven crew members killed is popular schoolteacher Christa McAuliffe, who was to have been the first civilian in space.

1988 Meryl Streep stars in *A Cry in the Dark*, a movie based on the story of Australian Lindy Chamberlain, who was accused of murdering her baby daughter in 1980.

1995 By ruling of the Supreme Court of the Philippines, Imelda Marcos returns to politics and wins a seat in the House of Representatives.

Imelda Marcos

1996 Seven-year-old Jessica Dubroff; her father, Lloyd Dubroff; and her flight instructor, Joe Reid, die when Jessica's plane crashes during her attempt to become the youngest person to fly across the continental United States.

1997 Eighty years after Frances Griffiths and her cousin Elsie Wright pull the Cottingley fairy hoax, two movies are made about it: *Photographing Fairies* and *Fairy Tale: A True Story*.

The world's oldest known person, Frenchwoman Jeanne Calment, dies at age 122.

1999 African American philanthropist Oseola McCarty, who saved a quarter of a million dollars working as a laundress then used the money to establish a scholarship, dies at the age of 92.

GLOSSARY

Adventuress: a female adventurer, daredevil. The term is often applied to women who have used dubious schemes or engaged in scandalous behavior to escape a background of poverty and lead a life of wealth and extravagance.

Amnesty: the act by an authority, especially a government, granting pardon to an individual or a group who have committed a crime, usually a political offense.

Annul: in marriage or other legal circumstances, to declare an agreement or law invalid. Unlike a divorce, which ends a legitimate marriage of some duration, an annulment is usually granted soon after the union and announces that it was void from the very beginning.

Blackmail: to demand payment or other service from an individual or group in return for not revealing incriminating information.

Burlesque show: theatrical entertainment popular in the late 19th and early 20th centuries characterized by humorous, earthy skits and sometimes a striptease act.

Cardsharper: a gambler who cheats at cards, usually a professional swindler.

Clairvoyance: the ability to perceive things by intuition or other means outside of the ordinary senses, especially the power to communicate with the spirit world.

Compatriot: a person who was born or lives in the same country as another.

Counterintelligence: an organized movement by an intelligence service to thwart the efforts of enemy spies who are seeking to obtain information or commit sabotage.

Courtesan: literally, "woman of the court." A woman who becomes the mistress of a man who is highly placed in society, especially a king or nobleman.

Debutante: a young woman making her formal entrance into society.

Espionage: the act of spying or employing spies.

Fence: in the criminal world, a person who makes a business of receiving and selling stolen goods. It is often more profitable for thieves to hand their loot over to an experienced, well-connected fence than to take the time to sell it themselves.

Forensic science: a science in which the circumstances of a crime are examined and the conclusions are introduced into the legal process. For example, a forensic psychiatrist might be consulted to determine whether an accused criminal is mentally fit to stand trial.

Fraud: the intentional misrepresentation of the truth in order to trick another person or an organization into surrendering a legal right or giving away something valuable.

Guillotine: an execution machine named after French physician Joseph Ignace Guillotin, who promoted its use during the French Revolution (although similar devices were used in other parts of Europe before then). The guillotine's heavy blade, with a sharp, angled edge, falls from a great height down two vertical guides to behead the victim lying, neck exposed, below.

Homicide: the act of killing another person. Also the person who commits the act.

Impostor: a person who takes on a false identity or title in order to deceive others.

Inquest: a formal examination of facts held by the coroner (a public official) in order to discover the cause of something, especially a sudden or violent death. Sometimes a jury is assembled to hear the evidence and pronounce a verdict.

Intelligence: in the world of espionage, the term "intelligence" is used in several ways. It describes the gathering or distribution of potentially valuable military and political secrets; the agency that collects this information; and the actual information that has been gathered.

Left-wing: liberal, that is, inclined to reform or make changes to the existing government's policies.

Litigant: a person who is involved in a lawsuit.

Manslaughter: the killing of another person. In legal terms, a charge of manslaughter warrants a lesser sentence than murder, because murder is planned ahead of time. The perpetrator of manslaughter acts on the spur of the moment, perhaps under great duress.

Medium: in spiritualism, a person who relays, or "channels," messages between the earthly and the spirit worlds.

Nouveau riche: literally, French for "new rich." The term is applied to people who have recently become wealthy and who are not yet welcome among the established members of the social elite. It is often used in a derogatory sense to describe a person who flaunts money or behaves in a coarse way that is associated with the lower classes.

Parole: the conditional release of a prisoner either temporarily or before the completion of a prison sentence, usually in acknowledgment of good behavior exhibited while in jail.

Phenomenology: literally, the study of phenomena, or observable occurrences. Philosopher Edmund Husserl is known as the founder of phenomenology, but others have expanded on or been inspired by his ideas. Essentially, followers attempted to examine and describe experiences without resorting to theories or relying on preconceptions. They tried to understand human consciousness by remaining self-aware.

Scapegoat: a person who is forced to bear the blame for offenses that were committed by others.

Séance: a meeting, usually led by a medium, at which people receive spirit communications.

Spiritualist: a follower of spiritualism, or the belief that it is possible for the dead to communicate with the living.

Theosophy: literally "divine wisdom." The term has been applied to several religious philosophies, especially ancient Asian belief systems, and was taken up by Helena Blavatsky in the 19th century. Theosophers believe that by embracing mysticism, direct contact can be made with God.

Treason: betrayal, especially the attempt to overthrow one's own government or harm a political leader.

Underworld: in mythology, the underworld is a realm deep below the ground inhabited by the souls of the dead (the Greeks called it Hades). By extension, the word has come to mean the criminal element of society, people who must carry out their villainous—or at least illegal—activities in secrecy.

INDEX

Numbers in boldface type indicate main entries.

CREDITS

Quotes

10 Blavatsky, Helena. *Isis Unveiled, Volume II.* NY: J. W. Bouton, 1877. **16** Calment, Jeanne. From Allard, Michel, Victor Lèbre, and Jean-Marie Robine. *Jeanne Calment: From Van Gogh's Time to Ours, 122 Extraordinary Years.* NY: W. H. Freeman and Company, 1998. **18** Cenci, Beatrice. From Shelley, Percy Bysshe. *The Cenci.* London: Reeves & Turner, 1886. **22** Crosby, Caresse. *The Passionate Years.* NY: The Dial Press, 1953. **31** Greenhow, Mrs. *My Imprisonment and the First Year of Abolition Rule at Washington.* London: Richard Bentley, 1863. **51** Méricourt, Anne Théroigne de. From Roudinesco, Elisabeth. *Théroigne de Méricourt: A Melancholic Woman During the French Revolution*, translated by Martin Thom. London: Verso, 1991. Used by permission. **60** Seacole, Mrs. *The Wonderful Adventures of Mrs. Seacole in Many Lands: Edited by W. J. S.* London: James Blackwood, 1857. **66** ten Boom, Corrie. *Corrie ten Boom's Prison Letters.* Old Tappan, New Jersey: Fleming H. Reyell Company, 1975. Used by permission.

Photographs

Abbreviations

AP	AP Wide World Photos
COR	Corbis
DOV	Cirker, Hayward and Blanche (eds). *Dictionary of American Portraits.* New York: Dover Publications, Inc., 1967.
HG	Hulton Getty
LOC	Library of Congress
MEP	Mary Evans Picture Library
MPI	Media Projects, Inc., Archives

9 (and 6) Anderson, Anna, HG. **10** Barker, Kate, LOC. **11** Bonny, Anne, LOC. **12 (and title page)** Borden, Lizzie, DOV. **13** Boyd, Belle, HG; Braun, Eva, HG. **15** Butler, Eleanor and Ponsonby, Sarah, MEP. **16** Caillaux, Henriette, HG; **(and cover)** Cannary, Martha, LOC. **18** Cavell, Edith, LOC. **20 (and title page)** Churchill, May, LOC. **21** Corday, Charlotte, LOC. **22** Crane, Cheryl, LOC. **23 (and title page)** d'Aquino, Iva, LOC; Darling, Grace, HG. **24** Devi, Phoolan, AP. **26** Duvalier, Simone, COR/Bettmann. **27** Ellis, Ruth, HG; Esther, COR/Historical Picture Archive. **29** Gaines, Myra Clark, LOC. **31** Godiva, HG. **32** Grey, Jane, HG. **33** Griffiths, Frances, COR/Bettmann; Gwyn, Nell, HG. **34** Hamilton, Emma, LOC. **35** Harding, Florence, MPI. **36** Hart, Nancy, LOC. **38** Hindley, Myra, HG; Humbert, Thérèse, HG. **40** Johnson, Claudia, MPI. **41** Jumel, Eliza, DOV. **42 (and 6)** Kelly, Grace, HG. **44** Lebrón, Lolita, LOC. **45** Lee, Gypsy Rose, LOC. **46** Lubetkin, Zivia, LOC. **47 (and title page)** Lyons, Sophie, LOC; McAuliffe, Sharon, NASA. **48** Macdonald, Flora, HG. **49** Marie-Antoinette, HG. **50** Mary, HG. **51 (and cover)** Mata Hari, HG. **52** Modotti, Tina, AP; Montez, Lola, HG. **53 (and 7)** Nesbit, Evelyn, LOC. **54 (and cover)** Onassis, Jacqueline, COR. **55** Pitcher, Molly, MPI. **56 (and cover)** Pocahontas, MPI. **57** Rosenberg, Ethel, AP. **58** Ross, Elizabeth, HG. **59** Schuyler, Philippa, AP. **61** Sforza, Caterina, MEP. **62** Silkwood, Karen, AP; Simpson, Wallis, HG. **63** Snell, Hannah, LOC. **65** Surratt, Mary, DOV. **66** Tipton, Billy, from *Suits Me: The Double Life of Billy Tipton*, by Diane Wood Middlebrook. **68** Van Lew, Elizabeth, Swem Library, The College of William & Mary. **69** Watson, Ellen, Wyoming Division of Cultural Resources. **70** Zane, Elizabeth, HG. **71** Héloïse, MEP. **72 (and 7)** Cenci, Beatrice, LOC. **73** Blavatsky, Helena, HG. **74** Fish, Marian, LOC. **75** Marcos, Imelda, HG.